Intellectual
Functioning
in Adults

Intellectual Functioning
in Adults

PSYCHOLOGICAL AND BIOLOGICAL INFLUENCES

Edited by

Lissy F. Jarvik
Carl Eisdorfer
June E. Blum

Springer Publishing Company, Inc. New York

Library of Congress Catalog Card Number: 72-77371
Standard International Book Number: 0-8261-1320-6

Printed in U.S.A.

Acknowledgments

The authors of Chapter 3 wish to thank, for their invaluable cooperation, the following: the twin subjects and their relatives; J. Allen, E. Knell, and M. Reiter for assisting in the psychological examinations; and F. Goldstein for administrative assistance in carrying out the field work.

The authors of Chapter 4 wish to acknowledge their appreciation of the assistance of Cornelia Service, Reesa Smith, and Susan Whittington.

The generous assistance provided by William A. Owens, Jr., and by the Institute for Behavioral Research, University of Georgia, Athens, Georgia, is acknowledged by the author of Chapter 5.

Drs. Frank Dalton and Wiley Bland, and Miss Reesa Smith are thanked by the authors of Chapter 10 for their assistance.

The author of Chapter 11 gratefully acknowledges the help of Drs. Obrist, E. W. Busse, and C. Eisdorfer for their contribution to the original collection of the data for the Duke Geriatric Project.

Preface

The contributions to this volume were drawn from selected symposia of the Division on Adult Development and Aging at the 76th and 78th annual meetings of the American Psychological Association in San Francisco (1968) and Miami (1970), respectively. These papers were chosen because, in addition to summarizing the results of significant current research, they may have clinical applicability as well. For this volume, several of the papers were rewritten and updated in 1970–71 to incorporate the most recent findings and to make the material more appropriate to a written rather than spoken format.

The interdisciplinary approach of this volume, incorporating psychological, biological, and life history variables, reflects the multiplicity of factors interacting in the production of age changes. Clearly, "agedness" is not synonymous with advanced chronological age *per se.*

The first section concentrates upon longitudinal research, an approach that has attracted but a handful of investigators in the field of aging. By offering the data of seven long-term studies of intellectual changes, Section 1 encompasses most of the follow-up research in this area. It includes the oldest existing developmental study on the young (Berkeley Growth Study) and the oldest ongoing project on the aged (New York State Psychiatric Institute Twin Study), thus covering the second through the ninth decades of life.

The four contributions to the second section examine some of the somatic correlates of psychological change and include data emanating from two of the few longitudinal studies available. Evidence is provided of associations between decline in intellectual functioning and elevated blood pressure, focal disturbances on EEG, and low cerebral blood flow. This section also includes the results of pioneer investigations relating physiological changes (cardiovascular, autonomic, and central nervous systems) to behavioral changes (reaction time).

A correlation between somatic variability and socioeconomic factors has been suggested by some of the findings reported in this section, but the unraveling of the complex interaction of somatic, cognitive, and social influences has been handicapped by lack of adequate information on life histories.

The third section thus represents a recognition of the yet untapped contribution of lifetime experiential variables to the physical and mental changes accompanying the aging process. The construction of a cogent life history interview necessitates steering between the Scylla of tedious codifiable questioning of the aged and the Charybdis of fragmentary unstandardized open-ended interviewing. Various modes of dealing with this dilemma are explored.

It is hoped that the research presented here on psychological and somatic changes in the aging may serve as a springboard for the future investigations so urgently needed in the field of gerontology.

We thank the contributors for donating their share of the proceeds of this volume to the Division on Adult Development and Aging (Division 20) of the American Psychological Association. We also thank Louise Bettner, Donna Cohen, and Connie Weil for their indefatigable efforts in helping to assemble this volume.

June 1972

Lissy F. Jarvik*
Carl Eisdorfer
June E. Blum

* The volume was completed while the senior editor was on leave holding appointments at the Veterans Administration Center for Psychosocial Medicine (Brentwood) and the Department of Psychiatry, University of California at Los Angeles; their cooperation is gratefully acknowledged.

Contents

PART I. INDIVIDUAL CHANGES IN ADULT INTELLIGENCE: LONGITUDINAL APPROACHES

1. The Institute of Human Development Studies, Berkeley and Oakland. *Dorothy H. Eichorn*[A] 1

2. The Age Center of New England Study. *Paul J. Rhudick and Chad Gordon*[A] 7

3. The New York State Psychiatric Institute Study of Aging Twins. *June E. Blum, Edward T. Clark, and Lissy F. Jarvik*[A] 13

4. Intellectual Changes with Advancing Age. *Carl Eisdorfer and Frances Wilkie*[A] 21

5. Life History Subgroups as Moderators in the Prediction of Intellectual Change. *Lyle F. Schoenfeldt*[B] 31

6. Personality Development and Intellectual Functioning from 21 months to 40 years. *Marjorie P. Honzik and Jean W. Macfarlane*[B] 45

7. Educational Experience and the Maintenance of Intellectual Functioning by the Aged: An Overview. *Samuel Granick and Alfred S. Friedman*[B] 59

8. Discussion: Patterns of Intellectual Functioning in the Later Years. *Lissy F. Jarvik* 65

PART II. SOMATIC COMPONENTS OF PSYCHOLOGICAL CHANGES IN ADULTS

9. Mechanisms of Brain-Body Interaction in the Aged. *William G. Troyer*[A] 69

10. Systemic Disease and Behavioral Correlates. *Frances L. Wilkie and Carl Eisdorfer*[A] 83

11. Cerebral Correlates of Intellectual Function in Senescence *H. Shan Wang*[A] 95

12. Relation of Increased Attention to Central and Autonomic Nervous System States. *Larry W. Thompson and John B. Nowlin* 107

13. Discussion: Mind and Body. *Carl Eisdorfer* 125

PART III. POTENTIAL CONTRIBUTION OF LIFE HISTORY APPROACHES

14. Design of a Comprehensive Life History Interview Schedule. *Lissy F. Jarvik, Ruth Bennett, and Barbara Blumner*[A] 127

15. Adaptability of Life History Interviews to the Study of Adult Development. *Majda Thurnher*[A] 137

16. Discussion: Potential Contribution of and Current Obstacles to the Collection of Life History Data on Aging. *Ruth Bennett* 143

PART IV. SUMMARY

17. A Summary: Prospects and Problems of Research on the Longitudinal Development of Man's Intellectual Capacities throughout Life. *James E. Birren* 149

REFERENCES 155

INDEX 173

[A] Based on a paper presented in 1968
[B] Based on a paper presented in 1970

List of Contributors

Ruth Bennett, Ph.D., Principal Research Scientist, Gerontology, Biometrics Research, New York State Department of Mental Hygiene; Adjunct Associate Professor, Program in Services to the Aging, Teachers College, Columbia University.

James E. Birren, Ph.D., Director, Gerontology Center and Professor of Psychology, University of Southern California; Editor, Journal of Gerontology.

June E. Blum, Ph.D., Research Associate, Department of Psychiatry, College of Physicians and Surgeons, Columbia University; Senior Clinical Psychologist, Department of Medical Genetics, New York State Psychiatric Institute; and Staff Member of the Research Department and the Adult Therapy Department of the Postgraduate Center for Mental Health, New York.

Barbara Blumner, M.A., Assistant Research Scientist, Department of Medical Genetics, New York State Psychiatric Institute (at present, Department of Biometrics, New York State Psychiatric Institute).

Edward T. Clark, Ph.D., Chairman, Department of Foundations and Behavioral Studies, St. John's University, New York.

Dorothy H. Eichorn, Ph.D., Research Psychologist and Administrator, Child Study Center, Institute of Human Development, University of California, Berkeley.

Carl Eisdorfer, M.D., Ph.D., Chairman, Department of Psychiatry, University of Washington, Seattle.

Alfred S. Friedman, Ph.D., Director of Research, Philadelphia Psychiatric Center, Philadelphia.

Chad Gordon, Ph.D., Fox Professor of Sociology and Chairman, Department of Sociology, Rice University, Houston.

Samuel Granick, Ph.D., Director of Research for Community Mental Health, Philadelphia Psychiatric Center, Philadelphia.

Marjorie P. Honzik, Ph.D., Lecturer in Psychology, University of California, Berkeley and Research Psychologist, Institute of Human Development, University of California, Berkeley.

Lissy F. Jarvik, M.D., Ph.D., Professor, Department of Psychiatry, UCLA Center for the Health Sciences, Los Angeles; and Director, Psychogenetic Unit, Veterans Administration Hospital (Brentwood) (Psychosocial Medicine), Los Angeles. Formerly at New York State Psychiatric Institute and Columbia University.

Jean W. Macfarlane, Ph.D., Professor of Psychology, Emeritus; formerly Research Psychologist, Institute of Human Development, University of California, Berkeley.

John B. Nowlin, M.D., Assistant Professor, Community Health Sciences, Duke University Medical Center.

Paul J. Rhudick, Ph.D., Staff Clinical Psychologist, Veterans Administration Hospital, Boston; Consulting Psychologist, Boston Hospital for Women; Lecturer in Social Relations, Harvard University.

Lyle F. Schoenfeldt, Ph.D., Associate Professor, Department of Psychology, University of Georgia, Athens.

Larry W. Thompson, Ph.D., Professor of Medical Psychology, Duke University Medical Center.

Majda Thurnher, Ph.D., Assistant Project Director, Human Development Program, Langley Porter Neuropsychiatric Institute, University of California, San Francisco.

William G. Troyer, M.D., Assistant Professor of Internal Medicine, University of Wisconsin School of Medicine, Madison; formerly at Department of Neurophysiology, Walter Reed Army Medical Center, Washington, D.C.

H. Shan Wang, M.D., Associate Professor of Psychiatry, School of Medicine, and Scientific Associate, Center for the Study of Aging and Human Development, Duke University Medical Center.

Frances L. Wilkie, M.A., Research Associate, Medical Psychology, Duke University Medical Center.

Intellectual
Functioning
in Adults

Part I
Individual Changes in Adult Intelligence: Longitudinal Approaches

1 The Institute of Human Development Studies, Berkeley and Oakland

Dorothy H. Eichorn

In relation to most studies in this volume, those from the Institute of Human Development are a temporal paradox. As longitudinal studies they are the oldest, having been in progress for over 40 years. Yet the chronological ages covered are the youngest: members of the Berkeley Growth Study and of the Guidance Study, for whom mental testing began at one and 21 months, respectively, are just about 43 years old; the average age of the persons in the Oakland Growth Study, who had their first tests at 10½ years, is approximately 50. However, the time span over which *adult* change can be traced, i.e., about 20 years, is similar to that in the studies of older persons being reported in this paper. In the Oakland Growth Study, Terman Group Tests

The author acknowledges Grant HD 03617–04 from the National Institute of Child Health and Human Development for support of the five-year generational study. The 36-year data collection for the Berkeley Growth Study was funded in part by MH 08135. Funding for earlier phases of the Oakland Growth Study came in part from the National Institute of Mental Health, the Ford Foundation, and the Laura Spelman Rockefeller Fund.

were administered at about 16½ and 33 years; in the Berkeley Growth Study, Form I of the Wechsler-Bellevue was administered at 16, 18, 21, and 26 years, and the WAIS at 36 years.

Although at present we can speak about age changes only from birth to young adulthood, our interest extends further. We have embarked on a five-year intergenerational study, funded by the National Institute of Child Health and Human Development, that includes tests at about ages 40 and 50 years for members of the Guidance and Oakland Growth Studies, respectively (the 36-year tests in the Berkeley Growth Study were completed several years ago), and at ages ranging from about 60 to 90 years for a majority of the parents of subjects (Ss) from all three studies. In addition, short-term longitudinal testing of the children of Ss from each study is under way—a long-term study of the children of the Berkeley Growth Study sample from age six months through 18 years has been in progress for some 19 years; children of the other groups were tested once during the late 1950's. To add to our credibility as longitudinal studies of aging, an original investigator from each group is serving in an advisory capacity. These ladies, who themselves range in age from almost 70 to the mid-70's, are theoretically retired, but in practice they are still actively working with data and subjects. If the second generation of investigators proves as durable and dedicated, we may yet have longitudinal data on change, intellectual and otherwise, from nascence through senescence and partway back again.

The issues that have concerned us—for example, differential patterns of change in terms of type of function and of the subjects' characteristics and life experiences, shifts in the interrelationships among abilities, and method-ological problems in the measurement of change—are common to all studies of intellectual change, regardless of the age span examined. This resume of our findings draws mainly on the Berkeley Growth Study because the intel-lectual development of that group has been most extensively assessed and analyzed.

That increments in mental ability occur during adulthood no longer seems debatable. The questions become: in what, for whom, and when? In the Berkeley Growth Study sample the overall trend from 16 to 36 years is an increase, although at a decelerating rate, for males, while females show a very slight decline after 26 years. No subtest, however, conforms exactly to this pattern. Taking the subtests in the approximate order in which they "hold up" with age, there are two—Vocabulary and Information—that show gains in both sexes through age 36. Vocabulary increases markedly from 16 to 21 years, little from 21 to 26 years, and again markedly from 26 to 36 years; while Information shows smaller but quite steady gains between each of the five testings. Four tests—Similarities, Block Design, Picture Completion, and Picture Arrangement—approximate the general pattern in that males gain through age 36, but females simply hold their own after age 26. On the remaining five tests, gains are confined to the earlier years in both sexes. Males do not improve in Arithmetic after age 26; females decline. For both sexes Digit Span decreases slightly—and Object Assembly considerably—after age 26. Digit Symbol scores increase only up to 21 years, then drop continuously for males; whereas among females there is no change from 21 to 26 years, with a decrease between the ages of 26 and 36. Comprehension scores change little after 18: females improve slightly up to 21 years, then decline, and males gain only half a point in the period from 18 to 36 years.

Over the entire age span from 16 to 36, males make greater gains on all subtests, although the sex differential is negligible on Information, Vocabulary, Arithmetic, and Digit Symbol. Because females in this sample start at a higher level on all subtests except Arithmetic and gain at least through age 26 in most, the net result at age 36 is approximately equal means for the two sexes. Exceptions are Vocabulary and Digit Symbol, on which females still score higher at age 36, and Arithmetic, in which they remain lower than males. The sex differences in size of gain is greatest for Picture Arrangement, Digit Span, Similarities, and Block Design, tests on which males make their greatest gains. Among females the largest gains are in Vocabulary, Information, Arithmetic, and Similarities.

All statements about gains in this study and in most others must be tentative because the tests lack adequate ceiling and, when there is a change in the form of the test, one needs data on relative difficulty. To cite only two examples, the relatively early cessation of improvement in Comprehension scores in our sample may derive at least in part from the fact that more Ss were nearer to the ceiling on this subtest than on any other. The smaller rate of gain in Vocabulary from age 21 to 26 than from 26 to 36 may be a function of insufficient ceiling on the Wechsler-Bellevue—the WAIS has many more vocabulary items.

Despite these reservations, we can say with reasonable confidence that gains are not simply practice effects, nor are they confined to persons of either high or low ability. Data on these points are important, for such questions have been raised repeatedly about results from longitudinal studies.

Among the 54 Ss who took the WAIS at 36 years were five males and five females who moved away before the age of 14. They had no experience with either the Wechsler-Bellevue or WAIS. Ten Ss selected from those tested with a Wechsler scale at all five adult ages were matched to the ten inexperienced Ss by sex, by IQ at eight years (or nearest tested age), and, when possible, by parental education. The mean differences between groups in childhood Binet IQ was .3; in WAIS point score at 36 years, it was .2. On the Verbal Scale the *in*experienced scored 3.5 points higher than the experienced; on the Performance Scale the difference was 3.7 points in favor of the experienced. These differences are equivalent to about 4 points in Verbal IQ and 5 points in Performance IQ. Obviously, there was no difference in Full Scale IQ. If the difference in Performance score is considered a real practice effect, then we probably must accept a sex-by-scale interaction. The experienced males averaged 8.4 points higher than the inexperienced males on the Performance Scale; the difference among females was one point in the opposite direction. Conversely, the experienced females exceeded the inexperienced females by 4 points on the Verbal Scale; among males the mean difference was 2 points in the opposite direction. On the Verbal Scale all subtest differences were in the direction of the group differences, except that inexperienced females scored higher (.8 point) than did the experienced ones on Digit Span. For males, all subtest differences were also in the direction of total scale difference, but those for Block Design and Digit Symbol were negligible (.2-.4). The most marked difference was on Picture Arrangement (3.8 points); this was the only Performance subtest on which the female difference was in the same direction: the experienced averaged 1.6 points higher.

The "constant" sample of 27 Ss who took all five Wechsler tests has also been used to assess the relation of gain to ability level. At age 16, their IQs ranged from 64 to 142. When the group is divided into a lower- and an upper-scoring subgroup for each sex certain trends emerge even though the subgroups are too small (seven Ss per subgroup, except for six in the subgroup of lower-scoring males) to yield conclusive results and significance tests have consequently not been computed. The most clear-cut difference between "highs" and "lows" is in the timing of gains. Both follow the general age and sex patterns described above, but the "highs" gain more before 21 and after 26 years, while the "lows" make the greatest gains between 21 and 26 years. As we have found so often, the trends are more definite for males. Between ages 16 and 21 years, the "highs" of each sex make greater gains than the "lows" on seven subtests, with a total point score difference of 1.2 for females and 7.9 for males. From ages 21 to 26, "lows" exceed "highs" on six tests in males (5.7 points), whereas the difference for females is in this direction on seven tests—but only by 3.4 points. After 26 years, the size of the difference within sexes is reversed. Female "highs" make greater gains than female "lows" on six subtests and by 4 points, whereas male "highs" are superior on only four tests and are only 0.5 point above male "lows". Indeed, from ages 21 to 36, male "highs" make greater gains than male "lows" on only two subtests.

For both sexes the total gain from ages 16 to 36 years is greater for the "highs" than for "lows". The former gain particularly in Vocabulary, but also in Object Assembly and Digit Symbol; the latter show greater gain in Similarities. Gains are about equal for "highs" and "lows" in Digit Span, Arithmetic, and Picture Arrangement. On the other four subtests (Information, Comprehension, Picture Completion, and Block Design) the direction of difference is not consistent. *In toto*, the mean difference between "highs" and "lows" of each sex reaches a maximum at age 21, and by age 36 declined almost to the levels found at age 16. Again, it must be remembered that gains by the "highs" from ages 21 to 26 years may have been limited by insufficient ceiling.

Corroboration that gains are not simply practice effects comes from adult tests on over 100 Ss in the Oakland Growth Study. Testing was less frequent, yet nearly all Ss showed gains in test scores. The Terman Group Test, administered sometime between ages 32 and 38, was given only three times during adolescence, and the last test with that or any intelligence scale was at age $16\frac{1}{2}$. Despite the fact that the Terman Group Test definitely lacks sufficient ceiling, 95 per cent of the Ss gained in score over the approximately 17-year interval, with an average increase of one year of mental age. More than half the gain resulted from improvement in Vocabulary scores; little or no gain occurred in subtests involving ingenuity or problem-solving. Among Ss who were interviewed in their mid–30's and who had taken the Terman both then and at age 12 years, gains on the Sentence Meaning subtest were slightly greater than those on the Arithmetic subtest. As in the Berkeley Growth Study, males gained more than females across this span of over 20 years.

Data from both the Berkeley and Oakland Growth Studies are also in agreement on the constancy of scores across time for general and specific abilities and on the types of subtests and personality characteristics associated with inconsistency. These findings are too complex to review in the time available here, but they may be found in the papers of Bayley (1966, 1968) and of Haan (1963).

SUMMARY

In the Institute of Human Development Studies, the outstanding characteristic of intellectual performance, at least up to the age of 36 years, is a gain rather than a loss in scores.

Males, who scored lower than females on all subtests except Arithmetic, showed the greater gains, so that by the age of 36 years the sexes achieved approximately equal mean scores on nearly all subtests. The exceptions were Vocabulary and Digit Symbol, on which females consistently scored higher, as well as Arithmetic, on which females continued to score lower than males.

Comparisons among subgroups indicate that the gains observed in these studies are neither a function of initial ability nor can they be ascribed solely to practice effects.

2 The Age Center of New England Study

Paul J. Rhudick and Chad Gordon

As medical advances serve to prolong life, more attention must be focused on the problems encountered by the older individual in his attempt to adjust to senescence. Research workers have attempted to deal with various aspects of aging, but the question that seems to have generated the most interest is that of intellectual functioning (Birren, 1968; Eisdorfer, 1963; Jarvik, 1967; Kallmann and Jarvik, 1959; Kleemeier, 1961; Riegel et al., 1967). It is commonly assumed that as an individual advances in age, his intellectual ability declines—an assumption that must be questioned in the light of findings that superior subjects (Ss) tend to increase in mental capacity during adulthood (Bayley and Oden, 1955; Owens, 1953, 1966; see also Chapters 1 and 5). Even Ss of average ability show stability rather than decline on tests devoid of a speed or motor component as late as their seventh decade (see Chapters 3 and 4). In fact, examination of individual scores by Blum and colleagues (1970) revealed that some Ss' scores remained unchanged, if not increased, after the age of 73 years.

The authors acknowledge the support of the National Institute of Child Health and Human Development, Grant 1735–03.

The above-mentioned studies utilized the longitudinal method. The results were thus derived from actual changes in test-retest performance and, unlike the results of cross-sectional studies, were not extrapolated from a single set of scores by assuming that prior functioning may be estimated from current performance. The present study, also a longitudinal one, seeks to add to the needed information concerning the components of intellectual changes among the aging.

SUBJECTS AND METHODS

The Ss were 86 normal aging persons (36 males, 50 females) drawn from a pool of 232 Ss to whom the Wechsler Adult Intelligence Scale (WAIS; Wechsler, 1958) had been administered. The subjects were selected because they took the WAIS a second time—the test-retest interval ranged from one to eight years. Their mean age at the time of the first testing (T1) was 72.26 years (range 58–88 years); at the time of retest it was 76.19 years (range 64–94 years). All Ss lived at home in metropolitan Boston, and were members of the Age Center of New England. These members were healthy, aging successfully, generally managing well; about 8 per cent were still working. Some of the Ss were self-selected volunteers; others were drawn from ward precinct lists by probability sampling as controls for a recently completed United States Public Health Service study. The average educational level of the sample was slightly below a year of college work. While the sample did include some blue-collar individuals, the group consisted primarily of white-collar and semiprofessional individuals.

In addition to the WAIS, each S completed the Minnesota Multiphasic Personality Inventory (MMPI, Dahlstrom and Welsh, 1960), the Cornell Medical Index (Brodman et al., 1949), the Leary Interpersonal Checklist (Leary, 1955), and a Current History Questionnaire, all of which updated social characteristics and personal information; finally, each S underwent a complete medical examination.

In light of the substantial time lapse between testings (one to eight years), an F test was performed, on the basis of splitting the study sample into three groups: (1) those retested within two years (N = 35); (2) those retested between two and six years (N = 30); and (3) those retested between six and eight years (N = 21).

In reporting the WAIS results, raw scores are used rather than standard age-adjusted scores (Doppelt and Wallace, 1955) because the present authors, along with Eisdorfer et al. (1959), seriously question the validity of the proposed norms; for when the age-graded scores are used, findings reflect huge gains over time with regard to Verbal, Performance, and Full-Scale scores, along with gains on all eleven subtests. To further illustrate this problem, when raw score analyses are discussed, references to what the normed scores might have suggested will be made.

RESULTS

When the means of the first test (Time 1, or T1) and the second test (Time 2, or T2) are compared in terms of raw scores, it appears that there are slight gains on Verbal, Performance, and Full-Scale WAIS scores during the eight-year interval (average four years) even though the subjects advanced in mean age from 72.26 to 76.19 years. When age-adjusted scores are used (Doppelt and Wallace, 1955) (see Table 2–1), the gains are somewhat larger.

TABLE 2-1. Comparison of Raw Scores and Age-Adjusted Scores

	Time 1		*Time 2*	
	Raw Score	*Adjusted Score*	*Raw Score*	*Adjusted Score*
Verbal	75.18	125.62	76.54	130.07
Performance	41.05	114.29	42.32	119.44
Full WAIS	116.38	122.27	118.99	126.92
Mean Age (in years)	72.26		76.19	

When the *S*s are divided into three groups according to the length of the test-retest interval (less than two years, two to six years, and over six years), there are no significant differences between the three groups on full WAIS raw score or verbal raw score; however, there is a significant difference between the groups ($F = 5.311$, $p = 0.007$) on performance raw scores, with most of the change occurring in the group retested within two years (mean *increase* = 2.485) and in the group retested after six years (mean *decrease* = 2.000). Inspection of the data reveals why there are no significant differences between the three interval groups on full WAIS raw scores. Cross-over effects have occurred, in that the shortest time interval group (within two years) *decreased* the most on verbal raw scores and *increased* the most on performance raw scores. This increase in scores may reflect the influence of practice. Furthermore, males dropped significantly on the performance scale, while females did not.

In addition to a direct comparison of mean test and retest scores, *change scores* (changes that took place from one testing to the next, T1 to T2) were computed for each individual and then averaged. The results were unimpressive: no significant changes took place during this period. However, since the standard deviations were high for the analysis of change scores (ranging from 8.19 to 11.97), the frequency distributions were inspected in order to ascertain the percentages of individuals manifesting the most change in *either* direction.

Overall, 43 *S*s declined and 40 *S*s improved. In particular, 34 (or 40 percent) of the 86 *S*s declined by more than three points on their raw verbal scale, while 21 (or 25 percent) increased their scores by at least three points. These are the canceling effects that resulted in the lack of significant change in verbal efficiency despite some major individual changes e.g., one *S* increased his verbal raw score by 23 points). Similar observations apply to the performance scale (in which 12 percent decreased by at least seven points, while 11 percent increased by at least seven points) and on the full WAIS (where 25 percent declined by at least seven points—in one case, 37 points; 20 percent increased by at least seven points—in one instance, 32 points).

Examination of the "improvers" and "decliners" indicates that the "improvers" were more likely to be females. Yet there were no age, education, health, or retirement differences. The "decliners" as a group had higher verbal, performance, and full scale WAIS scores at first testing, but the differences between them and the "improvers" were not statistically significant. Eisdorfer (1963) attributed a similar finding in his Duke gerontological test-retest sample to regression toward the mean.

Inasmuch as age, health status, and initial intellectual endowment accounted for little of the variability in IQ change, personality variables, as elicited by the Leary Interpersonal Checklist and the MMPI, became the focus of the analysis. In relation to the Leary Interpersonal Checklist, few changes occurred between test and retest on the 16 scales of this instrument. Further, there were few differences on the Leary Interpersonal Checklist between the "improvers" and the "decliners." However, a noteworthy trend was revealed when the 16 scales were compressed into a dominance vs. love polarity (Briar and Bieri, 1963).

Leary defines *dominance* as reflecting an intensity measure, and includes such factors as force, power, efficiency, and mastery. An excessively high score on this dimension may entail some elements of hostility, but none of the Age Center subjects reached this level. The interpretation of the *love* axis is that it contains such traits as nurturance and affective orientation toward others—a high score reflects a type of orientation that entails over-conventionality, overconformity, and even "weakness" (Leary, 1955). Some of the Age Center subjects' scores on this love dimension did border on the overconventionality (weakness) area. However, it was the "improvers" who tended to increase their dominance score over time and decrease their love score concomitantly; the converse was found for the "decliners." Thus, while it may be premature to infer that the "decliners" are less intense in their approach, or even overly compliant or weak in interpersonal relations, the MMPI findings tend to support this observation.

A comparison of the "decliners" and "improvers" on all the MMPI scales corroborates the Leary Interpersonal Checklist to the effect that the "decliners" may be experiencing interpersonal difficulties. The "decliners" perceive themselves to be more paranoid, more psychasthenic, and they are more anxious. They deny aging, admit to more psychological and cognitive problems, and, finally, consider themselves less spontaneous than do the "improvers." Some of these difficulties reflect interaction effects due to aging, for when the "older" and "younger" Ss are compared on the MMPI dimensions, the older Ss perceive themselves as more hypochondriacal in an effort to deny aging. Moreover, they admit to being more dependent than the younger Ss.

The younger Ss checked items that portrayed a profile characterized by more dominance, ego-strength, intellectual efficiency, and role-playing than was found in the older Ss; as in the Leary Interpersonal Checklist findings, the younger Ss seemed to be more intensely involved with their environment. The 86 Ss as a group scored within the normal limits of the basic scales of the MMPI, thus differentiating the group from a neurotic or psychotic population. However, here too, while the mean scores suggest overall normality, considerable variability is evidenced within scale and subscale scores.

The Ss are to be tested again to ascertain whether or not the specific personality trends hold up over a longer time span. The emphasis on personality factors is vital, since age *per se* seems to provide little explanation for the cause of changes in intellectual functioning. To explore this concept, F tests were performed by splitting the sample into five age groups, from youngest to oldest at first test (58–88 years), and then making comparisons at retest to discover if age at initial test administration correlated in any way with IQ changes. There were no significant changes on the verbal, performance, or full scale raw IQ; nor were there significant changes in subtest scores. Further, the five age groups did not differ on retirement, status, health score, or educational level.

A further analysis was performed by dividing the group into thirds on the basis of the attained raw full WAIS scores. The three subgroups consisted of *S*s whose raw scores were under 121, from 121 to 132, and over 132; there were no significant differences in IQ at the start of the study. Moreover, there were no significant changes in relation to age or subtest score.

Finally, while overall sex differences are not impressive on the WAIS, they are beginning to appear on the Cornell Medical Index and suggest some trending. On the physiological level, the females report significantly fewer respiratory difficulties, less nervous system disturbances, and less urogenital difficulties; on the psychological level, they report less fatigue, less anxiety, and less tension than males. Whether or not these health status changes will find expression over time and IQ functioning remains to be explored when additional retesting is performed. One indication that these status changes may affect IQ is the previously reported finding that males drop on raw performance scores over time, as compared to females. A confounding variable is indicated by the recently discovered trend toward lower admissibility of symptoms in females; most of the Age Center studies have shown that females consistently tended to score higher on the Cornell Medical Index than males. A resolution may occur when the results of the physical examinations are compared with the Cornell Medical Index.

Summary

In summary, 86 *S*s, male and female, between the ages of 64 and 90 were tested with the WAIS, Cornell Medical Index, Leary Interpersonal Checklist, and MMPI. Test-retest changes were minimal, despite the lapse of four years, on the average, between the two testings. There were, however, considerable individual changes in that 51 percent of the *S*s declined in IQ scores, whereas 49 per cent increased. Age, initial endowment, retirement status, health, and other demographic variables do not seem to be associated significantly with increase or decrease in IQ over time. Instead, much of the variation in raw scores can be attributed to personality characteristics. *S*s whose scores declined during the four-year test–retest interval seemed to have interpersonal difficulties; *S*s whose scores increased tended to be forceful, intense, and strong in interpersonal relationships.

3 The New York State Psychiatric Institute Study of Aging Twins

June E. Blum, Edward T. Clark, and Lissy F. Jarvik

Longitudinal studies of aging suggest a positive association between mortality and performance on selected psychological tests (Baltes et al., 1971; Birren, 1964; Goldfarb, 1969; Jarvik et al., 1957, 1962; Kleemeier, 1961; Lieberman, 1965; Palmore, 1969; Riegel, 1966, 1969; Riegel et al., 1967). The most recent follow-up of the earliest of these studies (Jarvik et al., 1957) is the theme of the present report.

SAMPLE

The initial sample of 268 twin subjects (*S*s) was selected for psychometric study from approximately 2,000 twins, over the age of 60, who were collected

The project was initially supported by financial assistance received from the Rockefeller Foundation (1945–1951) and the National Institutes of Health (1952–1959) by the late Franz J. Kallmann, and is currently supported by the National Institute of Child Health and Human Development, U.S. Public Health Service, Grant HD 01615, which is gratefully acknowledged.

for a long-term investigation of the hereditary aspects of aging and longevity (Kallmann and Sander, 1948, 1949). The *S*s chosen for psychological testing were residents of New York State or of immediately neighboring areas, living in the community (not institutionalized). They were literate, English-speaking (to avoid linguistic bias), white (only a few nonwhites in the parent sample), and in good health.

The 268 *S*s constituted 134 intact twin pairs, so that it became possible to evaluate hereditary and environmental influences upon intellectual functioning late in life. As reported elsewhere, hereditary factors still exerted a measurable effect upon intellectual functioning after age 60, as shown by the fact that the scores of one-egg cotwins were more similar than those of two-egg twin partners (Feingold, 1950; Jarvik and Blum, 1971; Jarvik et al., 1957; Jarvik et al., 1962). Even differences in education failed to extinguish hereditary influences (Jarvik and Erlenmeyer-Kimling, 1967), and as late as the ninth decade of life one-egg twin partners still resembled one another on certain tests of intellectual functioning (Bettner et al., 1971; Jarvik and Blum, 1971).

For purposes of the present paper the *S*s will be considered as individuals, disregarding the accident of their twin births. They closely resembled the total white population of New York State, 60 years of age and over, with regard to sex ratio (1:1.26 in the selected sample vs. 1:1.2 in the corresponding New York State population, 1940 census) and education (29 per cent had a secondary education or better in the initial sample vs. 27 per cent in New York State). With regard to occupation, farmers were overrepresented, reflecting the preponderance of *S*s from rural areas with stable populations (Feingold, 1950).

TESTING

Due to the advanced age of the *S*s, their purely voluntary participation, and the longitudinal objectives of the study, selection among the then available instruments was limited to those tests which would minimize tension, frustration, and the "testing" aspect of the examination. The resultant test battery consisted of five subtests from the Wechsler-Bellevue (Similarities, Digits Forward, Digits Backward, Digit Symbol Substitution, and Block Design), a newly designed, simple paper-and-pencil Tapping Test to evaluate hand-eye coordination, and the Vocabulary List I of the Stanford-Binet. The latter test was included because of its reported resistance to age effects. Initially, other tests were administered, but completed by too few *S*s for final analysis.

SUMMARY OF PREVIOUS FINDINGS

In 1955 there were 168 survivors and 100 individuals who had died since the study was initiated. Analysis of the psychometric patterns indicated the possibility of discriminating between the two groups on the basis of test scores. The 168 Ss who were still alive in 1955 had achieved higher scores, as a group, on each subtest of the initial test round (1947–1949; hereafter 1947) than had the 100 subjects who had died prior to 1955 (Jarvik et al., 1962).

In a more intensive investigation of the suggested association between psychometric performance and survival, the scores of the 78 Ss who had taken any of the subtests three times before 1957 were classified according to increased, decreased, or unchanged test performance (Jarvik, 1962). The increased performance for each subtest was defined as a score on the third testing that was higher than the highest score on the first two testings; decreased performance was defined a score lower than that achieved on the first or second testing. A third test score, which did not meet either of the above criteria, was classified as unchanged. Three tests (Vocabulary, Similarities, and Digit Symbol Substitution) emerged as potential discriminators of two groups—survivors and decedents.

The concept of "critical loss" was then formulated to test the assumption that those three tests did indeed discriminate between the two groups, the survivors and the decedents. It was defined empirically to include two or all three of the following: an annual rate of decline of at least 2 per cent on Digit Symbol Substitution, 10 per cent on Similarities, or any decrease on Vocabulary. In computing "critical loss," only those test scores showing decreased performance were used, i.e., where the third score was lower than either of the first two scores.

To determine the "critical loss" the third test score (T_T) was subtracted from the highest of the first two scores (T_H). The result was divided by the latter score (T_H) multiplied by the number of years (Y) intervening between the tests, as follows:

$$\frac{T_H - T_T}{T_H \times Y}.$$

To express the quotient in percentage, the result was multiplied by 100.

In 1963, Jarvik and Falek applied the criterion of "critical loss" to those

34 Ss of the 78 who, having completed all three tests on three occasions, had either survived their third testing by five years (23 subjects) or had died within a five-year period (11 subjects). At that time, 28 of the 78 Ss had to be set aside for failure to reach the five-year survival/death criterion. The remaining 16 Ss had to be eliminated because they were missing one or more of the scores necessary for the calculation of "critical loss." Only 1 of the 23 five-year survivors, but 7 of the 11 decedents, showed a "critical loss" (Jarvik and Falek, 1963). In retrospect, the two groups were statistically differentiated (chi square = 11.4; $p \angle 0.001$).

PRESENT FINDINGS

As of 1967, the remaining 28 Ss could be classified according to the five-year survival criterion (23 survivors and 5 decedents) for a final total of 62 Ss (46 five-year survivors and 16 decedents).

TABLE 3-1.   Survival After Third Testing Related to Specified Decline in Score on Digit Symbol Substitution, Similarities, and Vocabulary Tests

	Initial Analysis* Critical Loss**			1967 Analysis Critical Loss		
Survival Status	Two or Three Tests	None or One Test	Total	Two or Three Tests	None or One Test	Total
Five-Year Survivors	1	22	23(+11)***	4	42	46(+14)
Died Within Five Years	7	4	11(+2)	11	5	16(+2)
Five-Year Status Unknown	7	21	28(+3)	—	—	—
Total	15	47	62(+16)	15	47	62(+16)

  * Jarvik and Falek, 1963.
 ** Defined as a combination of at least two of the following: an annual decrement in score of at least 2.0% on Digit Symbol Substitution or 10.0% on Similarities, or any decline on Vocabulary test.
*** (+) not tested three times on all three tests.

Chronological age was not a significant factor in the relation between the psychological test results and survival, since the 42 five-year survivors who did not reach the criterion of "critical loss" were only a few months younger than the 11 deceased who did (75.4 years vs. 76.0 years). The fact that age as such is not a good predictor of impending mortality, or of generalized intellectual decline during senescence, has also been noted by others (Birren, 1964; Blum et al., 1970; Goldfarb et al., 1966; Jarvik and Blum, 1971; Sanderson and Inglis, 1961). In fact, Kleemeier (1961) and Lieberman (1966) postulated that the crucial dimension in psychological changes in the aged is distance from death. As a decline on timed motor tasks also failed to distinguish the survivors from the decedents, it is possible that such decline represents a general concomitant of aging, while "critical loss" correlates more specifically with brain changes indicative of impending mortality (Jarvik et al., 1957).

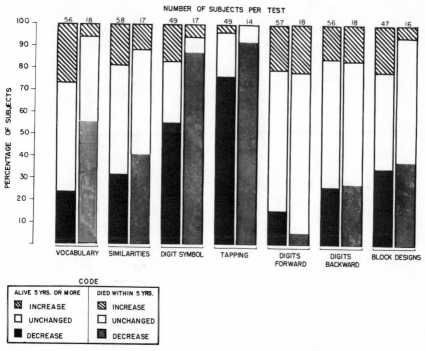

Fig. 3-1.   Intra-Test Change and Five Year Survival

When the scores of all 78 *S*s who took *any* of the seven subtests three times are examined (Figure. 3-1), the speeded motor task measured by Tapping still shows the most consistent decline regardless of five-year survival status.

The data were also examined in terms of mean scores, *eliminating the five-year survival concept*. The initial analysis (Jarvik et al., 1962) had revealed that the 1955 survivors (*N* = 168) had obtained higher mean scores on the *initial test round* (1947) than had the total original sample (*N* = 268). The

1967 survivors ($N = 32$), in turn, had obtained higher mean scores on every test in their third test session than had the group whose members ($N = 46$) died before 1967. The differences between survivors and decedents (Table 3-2) reached statistical significance ($p < 0.05$) on two of the subtests (Similarities and Digit Symbol Substitution). The *1967* survivors, at their third testing, also exceeded or equaled the original (1947) mean scores of the total sample ($N = 268$) on all subtests except Tapping and Digits Backward, even though at the time of the third test round they were on the average more than four years older than the original sample had been at the initial testing.

TABLE 3-2.   Comparisons of Mean Scores on Third Testing in Terms of Survival Status as of 1967 and in Relation to Initial Scores of Total Sample

Survival Status	Vocabulary	Similarities	Digits Forward	Digits Backward	Tapping	Digit Symbol Substitution	Block Design
		Mean Scores on Third Testing					
Survivors, 1967	29.6	10.7***	6.6		62.9	29.2***	14.6
N=32				4.1			
Age 73.7							
Decedents, 1967							
N=46	29.3	8.6***	6.0	4.0	57.5	23.2***	13.1
Age 75.5*							
		Mean Scores on Initial Testing					
Total Sample							
N=268	28.4	9.2	5.8	4.1	66.6	28.4	13.5
Age 69.7**							

  * Mean age at third testing.
  ** Mean age at initial 1947–1949 testing.
  *** Significant differences between groups (survivors and decedents): $p < 0.05$.

It is also noteworthy that this sample is an unusual one in terms of longevity. The subjects had already survived the initial testing by an average of eight years, despite the fact that the first testing (1947) took place after they had reached their seventh decade; the 1967 survivors lived an additional ten years into their ninth decade.

Summary and Conclusions

The 1967 follow-up findings support the previously formulated postulate, i.e., that a decline on certain tests of cognitive functioning (Vocabulary, Similarities, Digit Symbol Substitution) is correlated with mortality. By contrast, there appears to be an overall decline on speeded tasks (Tapping), which may represent a general concomitant of aging and is not a predictor of mortality.

Chronological age as such, while a variable to be considered, does not account for all senescent decline in cognitive functions; rather, certain psychological tests emerge as better indicators of the integrity of the biological substrate than does age up to 75 years.

In the present report, changes in psychological functioning have been studied only in relation to survival and chronological age. However, there are many other variables that must influence the psychological test performance of the aged. Follow-up investigations initiated in 1966 have been designed to encompass a broad spectrum of variables, including physical status, activity levels, chromosome constitution, mental functioning, life history factors, and socioeconomic conditions (De Carlo, 1971; Jarvik and Blum, 1971; Jarvik and Kato, 1970; Jarvik et al., 1971). Thus, the original collaboration between biology and psychology has been expanded to include the disciplines of sociology, medicine, psychiatry, and cytogenetics. Only an interdisciplinary approach is likely to yield further understanding of psychological functioning among the aged as well as of its relationship to the puzzle of longevity.

4 Intellectual Changes
with Advancing Age

Carl Eisdorfer and Frances Wilkie

The effect of advancing adult age on intellectual performance has been a topic of some interest in recent years. Numerous investigators (Bell and Zubek, 1960; Eisdorfer et al., 1959; Jarvik et al., 1962; Kleemeier, 1961) have suggested that the data reported by Kaplan (1956) and Doppelt and Wallace (1955) on the standardization of the Wechsler Adult Intelligence Scale (WAIS) for the post-maturity years should be subject to further scrutiny. Also of major interest has been the discrepancy in results between the cross-sectional studies that show an age-related decline (Doppelt and Wallace, 1955; Wechsler, 1958) and the longitudinal studies that have reported little age decrement in intellective abilities (Berkowitz and Green, 1963; Blum et al., 1970; Eisdorfer, 1963; Jarvik, 1967; Jarvik et al., 1957; Kallmann and Jarvik, 1959; Kleemeier, 1961, 1962; see also Chapters 1, 2, 3, and 5). Another relevant issue is whether the initial level of intelligence might affect the differential rates of intellectual decline among the aged (Bayley and Oden, 1955; Eisdorfer, 1963; Eisdorfer and Cohen, 1961; Owens, 1957).

The authors acknowledge the support of PHS Research Grant HD–00668 from the National Institute of Child Health and Human Development.

21

The results to be reported here represent the most recent findings on intellectual functioning among a group of relatively healthy community volunteers who were participants in a longitudinal, interdisciplinary study at the Duke University Center for the Study of Aging and Human Development. Although these subjects (Ss) do not represent a random sample, their sex, race, and socioeconomic characteristics approximate those in the Durham, N.C., area (Maddox, 1962). During the first ten years of this study there were four examinations separated by two- to three-year intervals. Each evaluation consisted of physical, psychiatric, psychological, and sociological examinations and various laboratory tests. Included among the psychological tests was the complete WAIS.

Based upon data obtained during the early stages of the Duke Study, several reports were presented which questioned the generality of the WAIS norms for older individuals (Eisdorfer et al., 1959; Eisdorfer and Cohen, 1961). In addition, Eisdorfer (1963) reported on the initial three-year retest evaluation; it demonstrated little overall decline, with the Ss tending to show minor changes in test performance in the general direction of a regression toward the mean.

METHOD

The testing involved 224 Ss in the 60–79 age range, 98 of whom completed four examinations during the ten-year follow-up period. Employing a cross-sectional as well as a longitudinal strategy, this report focuses upon the intellectual changes among the survivors of the ten-year study and also upon the intellectual performance of the Ss who were lost to the program prior to the fourth evaluation. In addition, differential rates of intellectual decline are examined as a function of initial intellectual level.

The results have been derived from three separate analyses. The first analysis examined the Full Scale Weighted scores from all Ss who had a given examination, regardless of whether or not they returned for subsequent examinations (i.e., Ss for the entire testing sample). In addition, this sample was divided into a Survivors Group, which included Ss who had completed the ten-year follow-up study, and a Non-Survivors Group, which included Ss who were lost to the program following the first, second, or third examinations. In the second analysis, a cross-sectional strategy was employed to examine the intellectual changes for the total sample across the ten-year period as a function of initial intellectual level. The third analysis focused upon those Ss who completed all four examinations during the ten-year period, employing a longitudinal strategy to examine the intellectual changes over time as a function of initial intellectual level. In each analysis the data for the 120 Ss who were initially examined in the 60–69 age range, and for the 104 Ss initially in the 70–79 age range were treated separately. The data to be reported in this paper consist of the Full Scale, Verbal, and Performance Weighted, and IQ scores.

RESULTS

Analysis I. The first analysis examined the Full Scale Weighted scores using both a cross-sectional and a longitudinal paradigm. For the Ss initially examined in the 60–69 and 70–79 age ranges, Figure 1 presents the mean Full Scale Weighted scores for the total sample, which includes the entire

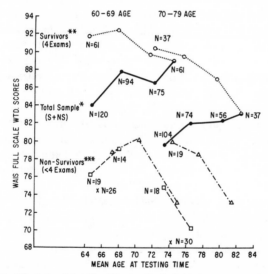

Fig. 4-1. The Wechsler Adult Intelligence Scale (WAIS) scores during a ten-year longitudinal study of individuals initially examined at ages 60-69 and 70-79.

*The *Total Sample,* represented by the solid line, includes all subjects (Ss) at each testing, *regardless* of whether they returned for subsequent examinations.

**The *Survivors,* represented by the dotted curve, includes only those Ss who had all four examinations during the ten-year period.

***The *Non-Survivors,* represented by the dashes, are grouped according to whether the Ss had only the initial test (represented by the X); tests 1 and 2 (represented by the squares); or tests 1,2, and 3 (represented by the triangles).

testing sample at each examination, independent of whether the Ss returned for subsequent examinations. Figure 1 also shows the Survivors and Non-Survivors, separately. The data for the Non-Survivors are presented in three categories according to the number of examinations they had: (A) only the initial test; (B) tests 1 and 2; and (C) tests 1,2, and 3. Since the scores are plotted according to the mean age of the Ss at each examination, it should be noted that the third and fourth examinations of the younger age group (initially examined at age 60–69) occurred at about the same age of the Ss as that of the first testing of the older group (initially examined at age 70–79). This results in the two curves overlapping between the ages of 72 and 74 years.

There was a positive linear relationship between the Full Scale Weighted scores on the initial examination and the survivorship of the Ss during the ten-year period. This was true of both the young and old age groups ($r = .20$, $df = 118$, $p < .05$; and $r = .28$, $df = 102$, $p < .01$, respectively), with an identical relationship significantly ($p < .01$) seen in the verbal and perform-ance areas. Thus, the Survivors (Ss who had four examinations) had markedly higher Full Scale Weighted scores than did their counterparts who did not return for all four examinations. The scores for the total sample fell between the scores of the Survivors and Non-Survivors. It should be noted that with repeated examinations the total sample becomes more similar to the Survivors sample so that they are identical by the fourth examination. In general, the Survivors tended to be more stable across the first three ex-aminations than the Non-Survivors, although both groups had changes in the same direction (i.e., increases or losses) between examinations.

Although the Survivors were not as labile as the Non-Survivors across the first three examinations, nevertheless, by the fourth examination the Survivors did show some loss from their initial level. Across the ten-year period, the Survivors who were initially examined at age 60–69 had a significant loss of 2.6 points in Full Scale Weighted scores ($t = 2.1$, $df = 60$, $p < .05$), which was primarily attributed to a 2.0 loss in the performance area ($t = 2.8$, $p < .01$). Over the ten-year period, the Survivors initially examined at age 70–79 had significant ($p < .01$) decrements of 7.3 points in Full Scale Weighted scores ($t = 4.0$, $df = 36$) and a 3.7 and 3.6 point loss in the verbal and per-formance areas ($t = 3.1$ and 4.4, respectively). Over the ten-year period, the older group of Survivors had a significantly greater decrement in verbal and overall Weighted scores ($t = 2.2$ and 2.2, respectively, $df = 96$, $p < .05$) than did their younger counterparts. It was interesting to note that between the first and fourth testing the younger group of Survivors (60–69 years) had gains in Full Scale, Verbal, and Performance IQ scores over time (mean increments = 8.4, 8.0, and 8.3, respectively) that were significant at the .01

level ($t = 10.2$, 9.1, and 8.2, respectively, $df = 60$). On the other hand, the older group of Survivors remained relatively unchanged in IQ between the initial and fourth testing, separated by a ten-year period.

Analysis II. The second analysis employs a cross-sectional paradigm. The entire testing sample was divided into low, middle, or high IQ group, based upon the *S*s' Full Scale Weighted scores on the initial examination, with each *S* retained in that category through subsequent examinations. For all *S*s the categorization was based upon the IQ equivalent of their Full Scale Weighted scores, using Wechsler's conversion table (Wechsler, 1955) for the 55–64 age group. According to this categorization the low group had an IQ equivalent to less than 85; the middle group had an IQ range equivalent to 85–115; and the high group had an IQ equivalent to 116 or more. It is important to note that these numbers do not reflect the *S*s' actual IQ scores at the time of the examination; rather, they enable us to evaluate all *S*s against the same-baseline categories.

Figure 2 shows the difference between the mean Full Scale Weighted scores at the beginning and end of the ten-year period for those *S*s in the low, middle,

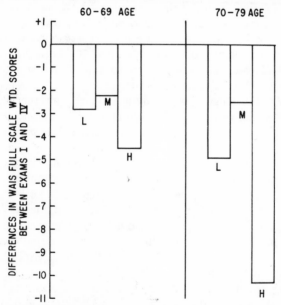

Fig. 4-2. Cross-sectional differences in Wechsler Adult Intelligence Scale (WAIS) scores between the beginning and end of a ten-year period among individuals initially examined at ages 60-69 and 70-79, with either low, middle, or high WAIS scores on the initial examination.

or high IQ groups. In this analysis, the results of the entire sample tested at test one and test four were incorporated into the analytic schema. Thus, for the group initially examined at age 60–69 years, there were 120 Ss at test one ($N = 40$, 59, and 21 for the low, middle, and high IQ groups, respectively) and 61 Ss at test four ($N = 13$, 33, and 15 for the low, middle, and high IQ groups, respectively). For the group initially examined at age 70–79 years, there were 104 Ss at test one ($N = 41$, 46, and 17 for the low, middle, and high IQ groups, respectively) and 37 Ss at test four ($N = 10$, 18, and 9 for the low, middle, and high IQ groups, respectively). The intellectual difference scores for both the younger (60–69) and older (70–79) age groups were obtained by subtracting the initial mean scores of the total sample (which included all Ss regardless of whether they returned for subsequent examinations) from the means of the fourth examination scores of the Ss who returned to complete the fourth evaluation.

For both age groups, in this analysis all three IQ groups showed some loss in the verbal and performance areas which was reflected in their Full Scale Weighted scores. At both ages, the middle IQ group remained relatively more stable over time than did the remaining IQ groups, with the high IQ group having the greatest loss. A comparison of the young and old Ss at each IQ level indicated little difference between the two age groups in the middle IQ range, while the older groups (initially aged 70–79) in the low and high IQ categories had losses of 1.9 and 5.9 points greater than that of their younger (initially aged 60–69) counterparts, respectively.

Analysis III. The longitudinal analysis included only the data from the survivors of the ten-year study and examined intellectual change across time as a function of initial test score level, using the three IQ categories described in the second analysis (above). Intellectual change was determined by subtracting the Ss' scores on the initial examination from their scores on the fourth examination. At each age level, Figure 3 shows the mean Full Scale Weighted score changes between the initial and fourth examinations.

Based upon a series of one-way analyses of variance, the results indicated that at each age level the low, middle, and high IQ groups had approximately the same magnitude of intellectual change over time in Full Scale, Verbal, and Performance Weighted scores. Although the initial level of intelligence was not related to the magnitude of intellectual loss over time, nevertheless at the younger age the middle IQ group did have a significant loss in the performance area over time (related $t = 2.1$, $df = 32$, $p < .05$). At the older age, the middle IQ group also had a significant loss in the performance area ($t = 3.4$, $df = 17$, $p < .01$) as well as in the Verbal ($t = 2.2$, $p < .05$) and overall Weighted scores ($t = 2.8$, $p < .02$). In addition, at the older age the

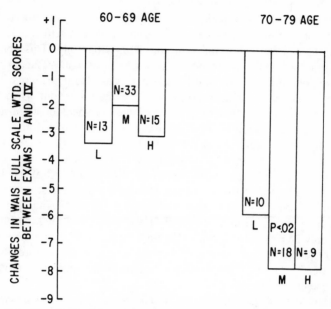

Fig. 4-3.   Longitudinal change (delta scores) over a ten-year period as measured
by the Wechsler adult Intelligence Scale (WAIS) among individuals initially
examined at ages 60-69 and 70-79, with either low, middle, or high WAIS
scores on the initial examination.

high IQ group had a significant loss in the performance area ($t = 2.6$, $df = 8$, $p < .05$). A comparison of the Weighted score changes between the younger and older Ss at each IQ level indicated that the middle IQ group at the older age had a loss almost three times as great as that experienced by their younger counterparts in the Full Scale Weighted score ($t = 2.1$, $df = 49$, $p < .05$). The old and young Ss at the low and high IQ levels did not differ significantly in the magnitude of decline over time.

CONCLUSIONS

Our results replicate previous findings in that our aged individuals who were able to complete a ten-year longitudinal study were functioning at a higher intellectual level than were their counterparts who were unable to complete this program. Viewed somewhat differently, the initial overall intellectual level of our subjects was positively correlated with survivorship (i.e., with continued participation in the study).

The total sample, which included the pooled scores of the Survivors and Non-Survivors, showed an increase over time, in contrast to the decrement noted among the Survivors and Non-Survivors separately. This appears to reflect a potential artifact in analyzing such data across time. The appropriate analysis of longitudinal data should use data only from the same subjects across time, whether Ss are lost secondary to death or drop out. The resultant analysis may in fact be that of a repeated measurement of cross-sectional samples (i.e., where the total N at each time slice is analyzed and the consequent slices compared across time). In this instance the Survivors were more stable and at a higher level than the Non-Survivors. Thus, repeated analyses of the total sample was increasingly limited to and affected by the superior performance of the Survivors. During the ten-year study there was a substantial loss of Ss, with the lowest IQ group sustaining a loss of 72 percent; the middle IQ group, a loss of 51.4 percent; and the high IQ group, a loss of only 36.8 percent. Thus, in the final stages of this study, the data are biased to the extent that a larger percentage of the initially more able (63.2 percent) were available for subsequent retesting than were the initially less able (28 percent).

The Survivors of the ten-year study who were initially examined at age 60–69 had a significant decrement over time in the performance area which was reflected in a slight but reliable drop in their overall scores. The Survivors first examined at age 70–79 had a significant loss in all areas.

The literature offers somewhat contradictory findings with respect to the relationship between initial levels of ability and the subsequent rate and magnitude of decline. At the more advanced ages there are few data available on people with superior or subnormal abilities. However, previous findings have suggested that through the mid-50's the initially more able remain relatively stable or show some gains—particularly in verbal abilities (Bayley and Oden, 1955; Gilbert, 1935; Nisbet, 1957). (See also Chapter 5). The data on people of subnormal abilities have been inconsistent (Bell & Zubek, 1960; Foulds and Raven, 1948; Kaplan, 1943; Thompson, 1951). The slight decline noted among aged individuals of average abilities has been somewhat less in longitudinal studies than that observed in cross-sectional studies (Doppelt and Wallace, 1955; Eisdorfer, 1963; Jarvik et al., 1962; Jarvik et al., 1957; Kleemeier, 1961; Miles, 1934). When examined longitudinally, our results support Birren and Morrison's (1961) findings that individuals at different initial levels of intellectual functioning (i.e., low, middle, or high IQ) sub-sequently maintain relatively similar patterns of intellectual change over time. Despite this finding, some of our IQ subgroups did have significant losses over time from their initial level. Thus, our Ss in the middle IQ range initially tested at age 60–69 years had a slight but significant decline in the per-formance area, while their older counterparts (initially tested at age 70–79) had a decrement in all areas. Our older group of initially more able individuals (high IQ) had a loss over time in the performance area. In contrast, our people with low IQ at both age levels had a slight but nonsignificant loss over time. Thus, the decline noted in the performance area among the entire sample (independent of initial IQ level) of Survivors first examined at age 60–69 could be primarily attributed to those Ss in the middle IQ range at this age. Further, the significant losses in all areas observed among the entire sample of Survivors initially tested at age 70–79 could be primarily attributed to those Ss in the middle IQ range, with the high IQ individuals also accounting for some of the decline noted in the performance area.

SUMMARY

In a ten-year longitudinal study, intellectual functioning as measured by the Wechsler Adult Intelligence Scale (WAIS) was examined in 224 com-munity volunteers in the 60–79 age range, 98 of whom returned to complete all four examinations during the ten-year period.

Longitudinal analysis demonstrated that persons with initially higher WAIS scores appear to show a better prospect for survivorship, and have more stable ability levels (at least on repeated WAIS testing). Certain IQ subgroups showed a slight, albeit significant, drop in intellectual functioning. This intellectual decline over the ten-year period appeared to occur primarily among our older individuals who initially functioned at an average or superior intellectual level (mean age at initial testing was 72 years; at the fourth ex-amination, 82 years) and among the middle-ability range of the younger Ss who were 64 years old at the initial testing and 74 years old at the fourth examination. The role of initial level of ability in survivorship and its relation to a possible methodologic error of repeated cross-sectional analyses over time are highlighted by these data.

5 Life History Subgroups as Moderators in the Prediction of Intellectual Change

Lyle F. Schoenfeldt

Although most of the early psychological studies of age differences were of a cross-sectional design, a number of longitudinal studies have been reported during the last several years (Bayley, 1966; Owens, 1953, 1966; Schaie and Strother, 1968). The first longitudinal studies were primarily concerned with changes in test scores over successive time periods, whereas recent studies have concentrated on the developmental correlates of age changes (Bayley, 1966; Owens, 1966).

The purpose of the present study is to examine the relationship between life experience and changes in mental abilities. More specifically, subjects (Ss) were divided into homogeneous subgroups on the basis of responses to biographical items. The resulting subgroups were evaluated by looking for evidence of differential age changes.

PROCEDURE

The Data

The *S*s were 96 males originally tested with the Army Alpha as entering freshmen at Iowa State University in 1919, and subsequently retested in 1950 and again in 1961. Each test session resulted in 12 scores for each *S* (including eight subtest scores), the three component scores resulting from Guilford's (1954) factor analysis of the Alpha, and a total score.

At the time of the 1961 testing the *S*s completed a Life Experience Inventory. The 82 continuum-type items (out of a total of 115) found to be related to shifts in test score over time were factor-analyzed by Gilmer (1963). Five factors were rotated to biquartimim simple structure (Harmon, 1960). The name of each factor and characterization of *S*s receiving high scores is indicated in Table 1.

TABLE 5-1.   Factor Descriptions in Terms of High Loading Items

Factor Name	*Characterization of High-Scoring Ss*	*Loading*
Socioeconomic Success (12%)*		
	Rate high occupationally	.77
	Hold a large amount of life insurance	.75
	Receive a large income	.74
	Have moved up occupationally	.67
	Live in a large city	.63
	Supervise people	.57
	Prefer to have many projects "in the fire"	.51
	Save a large part of present income	.41
Sensitive Intelligence (8%)		
	Upset by some tragedy in youth	.51
	Recognize a number of Alpha items from past	.48
	Frequently write down ideas	.42
	Tell jokes frequently	.42
	Devote much time to reading	.41
	Are sometimes tense and nervous	.40
Physical Vigor (8%)		
	Describe physical vigor as above average	.70
	Work not tiring	.49
	A typical day does not tire	.47

Have taken advantage of opportunities	.46
Concentrate on the technical aspects of music	.43
Rarely feel dissatisfied with themselves	.43
Feel more than adequate for their jobs	.40

Introversion (6%)

Do not particularly enjoy social gatherings	.50
Do not get together socially with business associates	.47
Feel people are not all good	.45
Did not live in rural area prior to college	.43
Consider themselves fairly tense or nervous	.43
Mother died at advanced age or is still living	.42
Prefer to work on one thing at a time	.41

Egocentric Independence (6%)

Consider own feelings before those of others	.54
Not engaged in social welfare activities	.46
Prefer to work alone	.44
Are less religious than the average S	.42
Frequently spend an evening in leisure reading	.41
Consider reading speed to be above average	.41

Note: Adapted from Owens (1966).

* Percentage of common factor variance explained. These figures should be regarded as approximate since the solution was not formally orthogonal.

Simple integral weights proportional to the magnitude of their factor loading were assigned to items, and a score was computed on each factor for all of the 96 Ss. Although the biquartimim criterion leads to an oblique solution, the factor scores were essentially orthogonal, with an average intercorrelation of .06.

Clustering Similar Profiles

Grouping. The factor score profiles of the 96 Ss were converted to an intersubject matrix of profile similarity, using the D^2 statistic proposed by Cronbach and Gleser (1953) as the measure of similarity. Subgroups were formed using the hierarchical grouping technique developed by Ward (1963; Ward and Hook, 1963). This procedure makes no assumptions as to the number of groups in the sample, but instead begins by considering each of the N profiles as a group of size one, and concludes with all the N profile in one group. At each stage, all possible pairs of groups are considered and the two most similar are combined, thus reducing the total number of groups by one while minimizing the increment in total within-group variability. A sharp increase in the incremental variability from a given stage to the succeeding stage indicates that the groups combined were dissimilar, and the pairings at the stage preceding the inflection become the solution.

Identification of misfits. One deficiency in the grouping procedure has been that, once assigned to a group, the individual remains in that group. Thus the assignment of individuals to subsets is usually less than optimal at the conclusion of the grouping (Ward, 1963).

A two-part procedure, described in greater detail elsewhere (Schoenfeldt, 1970), was employed to evaluate the fit of each individual to his assigned group. The net result was a set of unique groups, achieved by removing from the structure those Ss who did not fit any of the groups (isolates) or who fit several groups equally well (overlaps).

Analysis

Relationships between subgroup membership and age changes were analyzed both univariately and multivariately. The univariate analysis consisted of computing Newman-Keuls multiple-range tests (Winer, 1962) and comparing groups on each of the 36 scores (12 scores for each of three time periods—1919, 1950, and 1961).

Three canonical discriminant analyses were computed, one for each time period, using the eight subtests to maximally differentiate the groups that were identified. The canonical procedure examines the interrelations between the two sets of measurements made on the same Ss, i.e., the test scores and the roster of group codes. The discriminant function is that linear function of the tests which correlated maximally with the linear function of the group codes (Cooley and Lohnes, 1962).

RESULTS

The Groups

Using the procedure described, seven subgroups, including 84 of the 96 Ss, were formed. The subgroups ranged in size from 5 to 16, with the median size being 11. Of the 12 Ss not included, 4 were isolates and 8 overlapped two or more groups.

The following paragraphs provide brief descriptions of the groups in terms of personal data (Table 2) and the life history factors (Tables 3 and 4).

TABLE 5-2 Subgroup Differences on Personal Data

N	Group	College Major		Gross Income		Occupations
		% Eng'r	% Other*	% Below Median	% Above Median	
16	1	69	31	31	69	62% (10) eng'rs (6 with utility companies); 31% (5) mgmt
12	2	58	42	25	75	58% (7) sales/mgmt; 33% (4) eng'rs
12	3	84	16	25	75	67% (8) eng'rs
15	4	53	47	57	43	47% (7) eng'rs (2 profs); 40% (6) sales/mgmt
13	5	31	69	54	46	38% (5) sales/mgmt, 15% (2) eng'rs; 15% (2) farmers
11	6		100	91	9	55% (6) farmers; 18% (2) sales, 18% (2) teachers
5	7		100	100		60% (3) farmers, 20% (1) blacksmith; 20% (1) inspector
		48	52	50	50	
		$x^2=25.77$**		$x^2=20.90$**		
		($5df$, $p<.001$)		($5df$, $p<.001$)		

Note: The personal data were collected at the time of the 1950 testing.

* Of those classified "other," 88% majored in agriculture.

** Groups 6 and 7 were pooled for the chi square tests.

Group 1. This was the largest group (16 members), and differed from three, and only three, of the remaining groups on each factor. Those in this group had the highest mean on Socioeconomic Success (SES), majored in engineering, and tended to be employed in engineering or management positions. Of the nine persons employed by utility companies, six were in this group.

Group 2. This group of 12 was distinguished by the fact that it had a high mean on SES and the lowest mean on Physical Vigor. This group had the largest percentage (58 per cent) in sales and/or sales management positions even though slightly over half (58 per cent) majored in engineering.

Group 3. The 12 members of this group had the highest mean on Introversion and the lowest mean on Egocentric Independence. This group had the highest percentage majoring (85 per cent) in and employed (67 per cent) as engineers.

Group 4. Those in this group had a mean significantly lower than the remaining six groups on Sensitive Intelligence. Approximately half were engineers, with most of the remaining half reporting sales or sales management occupations.

Group 5. This group had the highest mean on Sensitive Intelligence, a very low mean on Physical Vigor, and a high mean on Introversion. Just over

TABLE 5-3.   ANOV *F*-Ratios and Newman-Keuls Analysis of All Ordered Pairs of Group Means on the Life History Factors*

	I	II	III	IV	V
*Factor Name***:	*Socioeconomic Success*	*Sensitive Intelligence*	*Physical Vigor*	*Introversion*	*Egocentric Independence*
F-Ratio***:	23.40	26.83	26.27	9.66	12.49
	*Grp. Mean****	*Grp. Mean*	*Grp. Mean*	*Grp. Mean*	*Grp. Mean*
	1 584 e	5 595 e	7 618 e	3 564 e	7 596 e
	2 552 e	1 557 e	3 575 ef	5 554 e	4 590 e
	3 549 e	3 545 ef	6 553 f	4 536 ef	5 549 ef
	4 526 ef	7 538 ef	4 549 f	2 496 efg	1 505 fg
	5 457 fg	2 478 fg	1 521 f	7 457 fg	6 554 gh
	6 391 g	6 451 g	5 416 g	1 427 g	2 549 gh
	7 290	4 362	2 364 g	6 414 g	3 396 h

  * Any groups having at least one common postscript following their respective means are *not* significantly different ($p > .05$) on that life history factor.
 ** Factors listed in descending order of common factor variance explained.
 *** All *F*-ratios were highly significant.
 **** Groups mean assuming the score of each individual standardized and transformed to the scale with mean of 500 and *SD* of 100.

one-third (38 per cent) reported sales or sales management jobs, two were engineers, two were farmers, and two were in the medical field.

Group 6. The 11 members of this group were over one *SD* below the mean on SES, they were low on Sensitive Intelligence, and had the lowest mean on Introversion, i.e., they were extroverted. Ten of the 11 majored in agriculture (36 per cent completed less than four years of college) and 91 per cent were below the median income.

Group 7. This group which was the smallest (five members), had a mean over two *SD*s below average on SES, over one *SD* above average on Physical Vigor, and one *SD* above average on Egocentric Independence. All majored in agriculture (only one graduated) and were below the median on income (average gross income was $2,200 in 1948).

The groups were necessarily well differentiated on the life history factors. The results of comparing the groups on each factor are presented in Table 3. These results are summarized in Table 4. As can be seen, each pair of groups differed on at least one factor, and all but pairs two and three differed on

TABLE 5-4. Life History Factors Which Significantly Differentiated the Subgroups; Summary of Newman-Keuls Result*

Group N	Group	1	2	3	4	5	6	7
16	1			Intro	Intro Indep.	Intro		Vigor Indep
12	2	IQ, Vigor		Vigor	Vigor Indep	Indep. IQ	Vigor	Vigor Indep
12	3	Indep.			Indep	Indep		Indep
15	4	IQ	IQ	IQ		IQ	IQ	IQ Vigor
13	5	SES Vigor	SES	SES Vigor	Vigor		Vigor	Vigor
11	6	SES, IQ Intro	SES	SES, IQ Intro	SES Intro Indep	IQ Intro, Indep		IQ Vigor Indep
5	7	SES	SES	SES, Intro	SES	SES, Intro	SES	

* If the group with the *smaller* identification number had the significantly *larger* mean ($p < .05$) on the factor, the name is placed in the proper cell *below* the main diagonal. If the group with the *larger* identification number had the *larger* mean, the factor name is noted *above* the diagonal.

two or more factors. The factors Socioeconomic Success (SES) and Physical Vigor provided the cleanest results in that each split the seven groups into three fairly distinct classes. On SES, groups 1, 2, and 3 were in the above-average class; groups 4, 5, and 6 were average; and group 7 was well below average. On Physical Vigor, group 7 was well above average; groups 1, 3, 4, and 6 were average; and groups 2 and 5 were below average.

Group Differences on the Age Data

Univariate analyses. A logical question one might ask with respect to each of the 36 variables (eight subtests, three components, and total for 1919, 1950, and 1961) concerns the degree to which the Alpha score distinguishes or separates the seven independently formed groups. The results of the 36 single-factor ANOVs comparing the groups on the Alpha subtests and components are presented in Table 5. Seventeen were significant at the .05 level or less. Newman-Keuls tests between ordered pairs of group means resulted in the differentiation of seven of the 21 possible unique pairs. As is shown in Table 6, all differences were between groups 1, 2, 4, and 5 paired with 6 and/or 7. In each case, groups 6 and 7 had significantly lower means.

TABLE 5-5.   Single Factor ANOVs Comparing the Seven Groups on the Army Alpha Subtests and Components

Subtest or Component	Probability Associated With Univariate F-Ratio		
	1919	*1950*	*1961*
1. Following Directions (R)		*	*
2. Arithmetical Reasoning (N)			*
3. Practical Judgment (V)			**
4. Synonym-Antonym (V)			**
5. Disarranged Sentences (V)		**	
6. Number Series Completion (N)	**	**	
7. Analogies (R)		**	
8. Information (V)	*	**	
Verbal Component		**	**
Numerical Component			*
Reasoning Component		**	
Total Score		***	*

*   * $p < .05$.
**   ** $p < .01$.
***   *** $p < .001$.

TABLE 5-6. Army Alpha Subtests and Components Which
Significantly Differentiate the Subgroups; Summary
of the Newman-Keuls Results*

Group		6		7
	Year	*Subtest or Component*	*Year*	*Subtest or Component*
1	1950	Disarranged Sentences	1919	Number Series Completion
	1950	Number Series Completion	1950	Analogies
	1950	Analogies	1950	Information
	1950	Information	1950	Reasoning
	1950	Verbal	1950	Total
	1950	Reasoning	1961	Practical Judgment
	1950	Total	1961	Verbal
	1961	Verbal		
2			1919	Number Series Completion
			1950	Analogies
			1950	Reasoning
3				
4	1919	Information	1919	Number Series Completion
			1950	Analogies
			1961	Practical Judgment
5	1950	Disarranged Sentences	1919	Number Series Completion
	1950	Verbal	1950	Analogies
	1950	Total	1950	Information
	1961	Verbal	1950	Reasoning
	1961	Numerical	1950	Total
	1961	Total	1961	Practical Judgment
			1961	Verbal

* The only differences were between groups 1, 2, 4, and 5 paired with groups 6 and/or 7.
In every case, groups 6 and 7 had the significantly lower mean ($p<.05$).

The results for total score, which were fairly typical, are plotted in Figure
1. As can be seen, the group and overall means increased during the 1919–1950
time period. The 1950–1961 patterns were more varied, although the trend
was to decrease slightly. None of the 1919 means differed. In 1950 group
1 differed from groups 7 and 6, and group 5 differed from group 6. Groups 4
and 7 were the only pair to differ in 1961.

Discriminant analyses. The univariate results (Table 5) indicated that 11 of the 24 subtests (eight at each of three time periods) differentiated at least one pair of groups. The disadvantage of this approach concerns the fact that the Alpha subtests are positively correlated. Thus, a pair of groups that differs on one test will tend to differ on other tests correlated to the first. To overcome this problem, three discriminant analyses were run, one for each time period. The seven groups and eight tests offer a natural application for DISCRIM, a procedure that is used to compute the linear combination (discriminant function) of the tests that best separated the groups. It is possible to get a better handle on the overall results by examining each DISCRIM to see which tests contributed most to the function and which groups were separated.

The 1950 and 1961 discriminant functions were significant, i.e., separated at least two groups, while the function using the 1919 tests was not significant (see Table 7). The correlations between the tests and the functions are presented in Table 7, and the group centroids are shown in Figure 2. The difference between Figures 1 and 2 is that on Figure 1 the vertical axes represent variations in total score. On Figure 2 each vertical axis is a different dimension—specifically, the linear combination of the eight tests given at that time period that maximally differentiated the seven groups. The average of all Ss on Figure 2 would be discriminant scores of zero for each time period. Each function can be named in terms of the tests that correlate highly with it, and these names are Verbal-Numerical Reasoning, G, and Verbal, respectively.

TABLE 5-7.   Test Correlations with Discriminant Functions

	Correlations with Functions		
Test	*1919*	*1950*	*1961*
Following Directions	.30	.43	.43
Arithmetical Problems	.13	.29	.57
Practical Judgment	.32	.45	.68
Synonym-Antonym	.37	.43	.68
Disarranged Sentences	.26	.62	.38
Number Series Completion	.72	.67	.12
Analogies	.57	.75	.17
Information	.56	.72	.37
Canonical r's	.59	.63	.61
Probability	.06	.01	.02
% Variance	20%	32%	22%

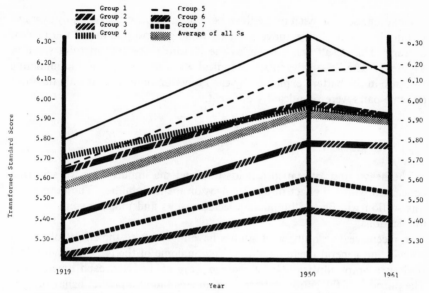

Fig. 5-1. Mean Alpha total score profile of each hierarchically formed group.

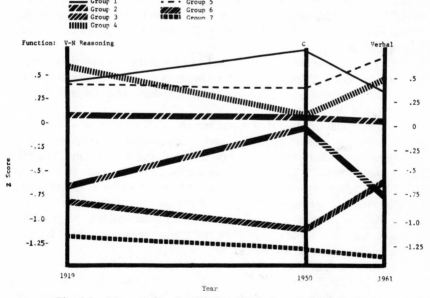

Fig. 5-2. Mean profile of each hierarchically formed group on three discriminant functions.

As can be seen, at each of the three periods, group 2 was essentially average, groups 1, 4, and 5 were above average, while groups 3, 6, and 7 were below average. This result was similar to the picture presented on total score in Figure 1. The relatively small canonical r's and percent of dicriminating variance in the battery explained by each function indicate that only the most extreme pairs were significantly different.

Discussion

The heavy dose of statistics tends to cloud the implications for scientists concerned with the effect of age changes on mental abilities. The purpose of this section will be to illuminate selected results and indicate some relevant implications.

In recent years a number of studies have investigated the effects of age on specific and general mental abilities. The outcome of the typical longitudinal study is a graph illustrating the average score of the *S*s at each time period. The purpose of the entire exercise is to understand and predict behavior. For example, if one were to generalize the results of the Owens (1966) study with respect to the total of verbal, numeric, and reasoning scores, the expectation would be that a current sample of Iowa State freshmen would score one-half *SD* above average, increase approximately 2/5 of a *SD* by age 50, and decrease slightly between ages 50 and 60.

The question this study has attempted to answer concerns the appropriateness of this "average" expectation for subgroups of *S*s. More refined predictions would be possible if subgroups whose members differ from the overall average could be identified.

This study demonstrated that it was possible to form groups well differentiated on the five life history factors, and to describe these groups in terms of the life history factors, college majors, incomes, and occupations. The relationships of groups to age changes were confined to differentiation of groups 1, 2, 4, and 5 from group 6 and 7. Thus the expectation for a current sample could be modified appropriately. For *S*s identified as similar to those in groups 6 (low SES and extroverted) or 7 (low SES and independent), the prediction would be that they would (a) be below the average mental ability of the total sample, and (b) increase less by age 50.

In his 1966 article, Owens described eight criteria as difference scores on V, N, R, and total score for the periods 1919–1950 and 1950–1961. These criteria were correlated with each of the five life history factors, with the result being that six of the 40 r's were above .30, or, more specifically, one r in the

60's, two in the 50's, and three in the 30's (Owens, 1966, Table 7). The present groups have not lost any of that strength of relationship, and very well may have enhanced it.

The major gain was in the comprehension of relationships. The question answered was *not* one of the relationship between traits and score changes, but rather concerned the types of people age treated kindly and unkindly at what time and with respect to what functions. The two groups distinguished by their exceptionally low scores on SES, groups 6 and 7, were also generally lowest at all three points on the Alpha scores. One group, No. 5, was well differentiated from groups 6 and 7 on several Alpha subtests and components, but was adjacent on the SES factor. The explanation was the fact that group 5 had a lower mean on the Physical Vigor factor.

It should be realized that the relationships are retrospective in that the life history data were collected in 1961. A number of items dealt with events that occurred much earlier in the lives of the *S*s, and responses were influenced to an unknown extent by the effects of selective memory. In this respect, collecting experiential data appropriate to the age of the *S*s at each testing would provide a better indication of the correlates (and perhaps causes) of mental changes. It is hoped that those who are now collecting such data will view the present research as suggestive of a viable approach that they might apply.

SUMMARY

The purpose of this study was to group or cluster life history profiles and then to describe the clusters in terms of test data collected over a 42-year period. The conclusions are as follows:

1. The hierarchical grouping procedure was effective in partitioning this sample into demonstrable differing subgroups.

2. The seven groups formed by the hierarchical procedure were most clearly distinguished on the Socioeconomic and Physical Vigor factors, each of which split the groups into three fairly distinct (high, average, and low) classes. Of the 21 unique pairs of groups formed from the original seven, 20 differed simultaneously on two or more of the life history factors; groups 2 and 3 differed only on Physical Vigor.

3. When the independently formed life history subgroups were examined with respect to differences on the Alpha scores, the consistent trend was for groups 6 and 7 to be lower than the remaining groups, irrespective of the test or the time period (1919, 1950, or 1961). Thus, for new *S*s identified as similar

to those in group 6 (low SES and extroverted) or 7 (low SES and independent), the expectation would be that they would start below average and increase less.

The hierarchical grouping procedure is suggested as a method of partitioning a sample of subject profiles into homogeneous subgroups. The result of relating the groups to the mental change data is an improvement in comprehension and prediction by permitting modifications of expectations (age changes in ability) on the basis of previous behavior (life history).

6 Personality Development and Intellectual Functioning from 21 Months to 40 Years

Marjorie P. Honzik and Jean W. Macfarlane

Nothing is more conducive to tempering one's confidence in ability to predict than being involved in a research project that has followed the same persons from infancy to age 40 years. One is forced to discard many "bright hunches," good hypotheses, confident predictions, and discover things never considered but which *post facto* appear quite reasonable.

Perhaps the most germane introduction to this paper is to give an excerpt from a subject's (*S*'s) life record that has direct relevance to the topic of "Personality and Intelligence."

One of the *S*s, at age 30, was a bright, articulate, talented, prize-winning architect, the father of two bright children. Our early records through his preschool and grade and high school years showed him to be a toneless,

The authors acknowledge the support of grants from the Rockefeller and Ford Foundations and USPHS grants MH 6238, 8135, and 5300 and HD 03617 to the Institute of Human Development, University of California.

inarticulate, withdrawn child, held over several terms in school, and graduating from high school without adequate college recommendation. He had consistently obtained relatively low IQs through the age of 18. To quote him at age 30: "You have to admit I was a listless odd ball." While we were trying to ferret out with him, in a long series of interviews, the many factors he felt were associated with the marked changes from his first twenty years, he interrupted to say, "You personality birds could profit from an intensive art course in design. You would discover that what makes a good design—and the possibilities are almost infinite—is that combination of atypical or offbeat elements which grabs one's attention and enough compensating strengths to hold the total in balance, even precarious balance. People, too, come in an almost infinite variety of designs with unique individuality and compensating balancing strengths, which, in my case, were very slow in developing."

His history, and those of other Ss which were not in accord with early expectancies, make us wonder at times if detailed biographies, with emphasis intra–individual coherence and change, are not the best way to contribute to valid knowledge in the field of human development. But, in addition to the case history approach, we have followed the conventional route in the search for stable group relationships between variables, and configurations of variables, across and through time, that meet appropriate significance levels. We will present some of these in this paper.

In 1948 we reported on the stability and variability of mental test performance over the first 18 years for a cohort of children born in Berkeley in 1928 and 1929 (Honzik, et al., 1948). The sample, selected from the birth certificate registry, was representative of this urban community at that time. (We should add that a Berkeley sample selected today in the same way would differ in many respects from that selected 40 years ago.)

These children, as members of the Guidance Study, were given fifteen individual mental tests between the ages of 21 months and 18 years. The tests used were the California Preschool Scales; Revisions of the Stanford-Binet; and the Wechsler-Bellevue at 18 years. Correlations were as high as .92 for adjacent age periods, but decreased markedly with the interval between tests, so that we found barely positive correlations between the tests given at 21 months and 18 years. Prediction from the 3-year test was higher and statistically significant. With each passing year, the prediction of the 18-year IQ increased. The results for this group are similar to those found in a number of other longitudinal studies: Bayley (1949) for the Berkeley Growth Study sample; Sontag, et al. (1958) for the Fels group; and Ebert and Simmons (1943) for a Cleveland sample.

Subjects in the Guidance Study are now aged 40 and have recently taken the Wechsler Adult Intelligence Scale. How well did these 50 men and 60 women maintain their relative positions over the 22 years? The correlations between the 18-year Wechsler-Bellevue IQs and the 40-year WAIS IQs are .74 for the men and .75 for the women. Correlations between the 6-year Stanford-Binet IQ and the 40-year WAIS IQs are .60 for both males and females, suggesting considerable stability over a 34-year period.

The Verbal IQ is relatively more stable over the age period 18 to 40 ($r = .69$ for men and .78 for women) than the Performance IQ ($r = .58$ for men and .62 for women). The most stable subtest is Vocabulary, where the r is .76 for men and .71 for women. The largest sex difference occurred on the short memory test, Digit Span, where the r is .75 for the women but only .51 for the men. One S suggested that this sex difference might be related to the differential occupational demands for certain men who have had to improve their short memory span, e. g., policemen, salesmen, etc.

Our second question is concerned with the gains and losses in IQ over the 22-year period. The average IQ at age 18 was 119 on the Wechsler-Bellevue; at 40, 122.8 on the WAIS. This represents a highly significant gain of 3.8 IQ points.* This study does not indicate the age when the peak in IQ occurs. Nancy Bayley's data for the smaller, more intensively tested Berkeley Growth Study sample suggest that the decline in the Full Scale IQ begins in the late 30's (Bayley, 1968). Despite the substantial gains in IQ, both men and women did significantly less well on the Digit Symbol subtest at age 40 than at age 18. This is a speed test and the difference suggests a significant loss of speed, and perhaps interest, in this type of test. The sex differences are generally more marked than expected. Both men and women showed marked and significant gains in Performance IQ, but only the women showed a highly significant gain in Verbal IQ. This gain, and the girls' gain in Arithmetic, is in part a function of the girls' relatively low scores at the age of 18. In late adolescence the girls were cooperative, but as a group they were far more concerned about social skills than about intellectual achievement.

Figure 1 shows the gains in IQ in relation to the 18-year IQs. The greatest gains occurred for the group of men and women with *average IQs*, while the sex difference is most marked for the "bright normals" (IQ range 110–119). The average gain for the "bright normal" women is substantial; the men's

---

* An unpublished study by Rabourn (1957) reports that the WAIS yields a lower Full Scale IQ than the Wechsler-Bellevue for a sample of 50 high school graduates with an average age of 20 years. This finding adds to the significance of the difference found in the present study.

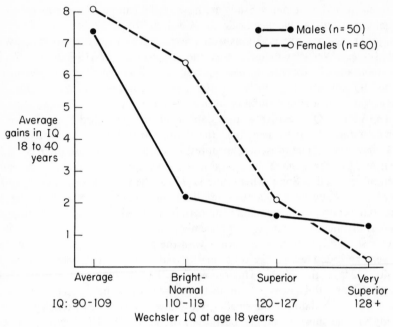

Fig. 6-1.   Gains in IQ between the ages of 18 and 40 years.

is more moderate. The most important finding shown in this figure is the generality of the IQ gains at all ability levels, probably due in part to increased experience—e.g., information, comprehension, and vocabulary—but it may also be due to an increased ability to profit by experience.

How would we characterize the 110 adults tested at age 40? The occupations of the men cover a wide range—from trucker to the professions of law and medicine. While the exact earnings of this group have not been ascertained, they are probably above the national average. When the Ss were born, their parents were earning less than the national average but were more educated. Three men and three women Ss have Ph.D's or M.D's, but most of the women are homemakers who come in saying that their teen-aged children know more than they do and that their own intelligence has probably sagged with disuse. Many of the men also believe that their children are more competent than they are; but the test scores of their teen-aged children are simply not as high on the average as those of the 40-year-old parents. Six Ss never married; 8 are divorced and have not remarried. The remaining 96 are married and have an average of almost three children per family.

What are the characteristics of those who have gained or lost relative to the norm? The scores of 16 men and 11 women were lower on the WAIS at age 40 than on the Wechsler-Bellevue at age 18. We find in this group Ss who had accidents or illnesses involving the central nervous system resulting in specific deficits; individuals who are depressed; others who are chronically fatigued; and alcoholics. But all are functioning, after a fashion, in the community. Many of the small IQ changes represent, of course, errors of measurement, regression to the mean, or variations due to changes in interest, mood, or cooperation.

Fairly substantial increases in IQ occurred in the four who have Ph.D's and in four of the six who never married. In general, the education of the gainers was superior to the remaining study members, but the average difference in years of schooling between the gainers and the rest of the sample is only half a year for both men and women. However, a larger proportion of the gainers obtained degrees from high-ranking universities in contrast to junior colleges; and three of the women lived in Europe for extended periods of time. Among the non-gainers were the top three popularity idols of the school years, whose talents, abilities, and drives were devoted to pursuing social skills and not to the internalizing, hair-splitting thinking that helps to raise scores on mental tests.

A major focus of the Guidance Study has been the personality development of these normal men and women. Interviews with the parents began when the subjects were aged 21 months, and continued on a yearly basis until they were 17 years old. Interviews with the teachers about the Ss' behavior occurred yearly, from kindergarten to 10th grade; and the children themselves were interviewed at half-yearly intervals between the ages of 6 and 17. These interviews have been rated and coded as they were taken, and at some later time we hope to relate these ratings to intellectual functioning. For purposes of the present report, we used case Q-sort evaluations in relation to IQ gains during adulthood and at age 40 years.

The Q-sort, consisting of 100 personality items, is designed to measure within-person or ipsative rankings of characteristics on a 9-point scale (Block, 1961). Each subject's case file from birth to age 18 was sorted for these 100 items. In an attempt to find those personality characteristics in children which might predict gains in IQ during the adult years, we compared those whose IQs increased between the ages of 18 and 40 with the remainder of the sample for all 100 Q-sort items. Data for men and women were analyzed separately. Table 1 shows that few significant differences emerged. However, certain consistencies suggest that the findings are not all chance ones. The men (7) and women (13) who gained the most (8 or more IQ points) were judged as

TABLE 6-1. Q-Sort Personality Characteristics Of Persons Gaining In IQ Between 18 And 40 Years, As Compared With Remainder Of Group

	Age Period Personality Rated			
Q-Sort Personality Characteristics	21 mos.-18 years		30 years	
	Males	Females	Males	Females
t tests significant for both males and females	t	t	t	t
28 Tends to arouse liking and acceptance in people	−1.7*	−2.1**	−2.7**	−.6
29 Is turned to for advice and reassurance	− .3	−1.6	−2.9***	−2.6**
54 Gregarious; emphasizes being with others	−2.6**	−2.1**	−1.4	.5
93 Behaves in a sex-appropriate manner	−2.3**	−2.2**	−2.1**	0.0
31 Is satisfied with physical appearance	− .8	−1.2	−1.9*	−3.0***
t tests significant for males but not females				
16 Is introspective	1.7*		2.7**	
26 Is productive; gets things done	−1.4		−2.2**	
33 Is calm, relaxed in manner	− .5		−2.0**	
66 Enjoys and reacts to esthetic impressions	.7		2.2**	
68 Is basically anxious	− .6		2.4**	
78 Feels cheated and victimized by life	.8		2.1**	
79 Tends to ruminate and have preoccupying thoughts	2.9***		1.8*	
84 Is cheerful	− .9		−2.2**	
92 Has social poise and presence	−.02		−2.2**	
t tests significant for females but not males				
35 Has warmth; is compassionate		−2.4**		− .6
55 Is self-defeating		2.1**		.1
74 Feels satisfied with self		− .3		−2.6**
81 Is physically attractive; good looking		−1.4		−2.1**
88 Is personally charming		−2.1**		− .6

Note: A negative *t* indicates that the gainers are *less* likely to show the characteristic than the remainder of the group.

  * $p < .10$ level.
  ** $p < .05$ level.
  *** $p < .01$ level.

characteristically *not gregarious* as children. For both men and women, this difference is significant at the .05 level. A second significant difference was one indicating that the men and women who gained were less extreme in the Q-sort appraisals of masculinity and femininity than was true for the remainder of the group. This latter finding was been reported previously by Maccoby

(1966). The only other item that was differentiating at a statistically significant level suggests that the Ss whose IQs increased were less likely in childhood to be among those who *aroused liking and acceptance.*

A more recent Q-sort was done on these Ss when they were aged 30 years on the basis of intensive interview material. These 30-year Q-sorts were performed independently of the data collected during the first 18 years. Since the 30-year Q-sorts were obtained in the middle of the 22-year span between the 18- and 40-year tests, we thought it might yield clues as to the adult personality characteristics of those whose IQs increased. We again compared the gainers with the remainder of the group. Two items showed significant differences for both males and females: at 30 years, the Ss whose IQs increased little or none between 18 and 40 years tended to be *more satisfied with their physical appearance* and were *more likely to be turned to for advice and reassurance* than was true of the IQ gainers.

Table 1 shows that a larger proportion of the 30-year Q-sort items were differentiating for the men than for the women. Two items that were significantly differentiating for men at both the childhood and 30-year evaluations were: *introspective* and *tends to ruminate and have preoccupying thoughts.* Other characteristics of the men at age 30 who were gaining in IQ were: *is basically anxious, feels cheated and victimized by life* but *enjoys and reacts to esthetic impressions.* In contrast to these serious—almost gloomy—characteristics of the gainers, the men who showed little or no gains in IQ on the Wechsler tests during adulthood were more likely, at a statistically significant level, to be *cheerful, calm and relaxed in manner, socially at ease, productive and gets things done,* and, finally, *likely to arouse liking and acceptance in people.*

Women who gained in IQ in adulthood tended to be *self-defeating in childhood,* while women who showed little or no gain in IQ in adulthood were more likely than the gainers to be rated *physically attractive, personally charming, feels satisfied with self,* and *has warmth, is compassionate.*

Although the differentiating items for males and females are not the same, a common trend is observable among all Ss whose IQs increase as adults. They tend to maintain distance from other people; they are likely to turn inward, not out toward people; and there is some evidence of a lack of nurturance in relation to others. It is difficult to know whether the gainers' seeming lack of, or concern about, physical attractiveness is based in fact or whether it is secondary to a withdrawing, and perhaps somber, mien.

Thus far we have contrasted the Q-sort characteristics of those who gained substantially in IQ between 18 and 40 years with those in the remainder of the group. Table 2 presents the statistically significant correlations between

TABLE 6-2. Relation of 40–Year IQs To Q-Sort Personality Characteristics Rated For First 18 Years And At Age 30 Years

Q-Sort Personality Characteristics	*Age Period Personality Rated*			
	21 mos.-18 years		*30 years*	
	Males	*Females*	*Males*	*Females*
Correlations significant for both males and Females	r	r	r	r
8 Appears to have a high degree of intellectual capacity	.73***	.67***	.62***	.56***
98 Is verbally fluent; can express ideas well	.51***	.38**	.34*	.33**
51 Genuinely values intellectual and cognitive matters	.51***	.51***	.33*	.40**
71 Has high aspiration level for self	.28*	.38**	.33*	.35**
83 Able to see to the heart of important problems	.45***	.53***	.11	.13
90 Is concerned with philosophical problems	.20	.30*	.42**	.31*
24 Prides self on being objective, rational	.34*	.38**	.10	.18
9 Is comfortable with uncertainty and complexities	.44**	.31	.27	.08
21 Does not arouse nurturant feeling in others	.28*	.51***	.25	.15
47 Tends to feel guilty	.02	.39**	.36*	.15
Correlations significant for males but not females				
16 Is introspective	.27		.41**	
31 Not satisfied with physical appearance	.06		.47**	
56 Not responsive to humor	.06		.41**	
60 Has insight into own motives and behavior	.36**		.06	
79 Tends to ruminate and have persistent, preoccupying thoughts	.15		.40**	
84 Not cheerful	.20		.51***	
86 Does not handle anxiety and conflicts by repressive or dissociative tendencies	.16		.40**	
Correlations significant for females but not males				
3 Has a wide range of interests		.42***		.38**
26 Is productive; gets things done		.41***		.07
61 Does not create and exploit dependency in people		−.01		.34**
66 Enjoys esthetic impressions; esthetically reactive		.37**		.15
87 Interprets basically simple situations in complicated ways		.32**		−.07
72 Overconcerned with own adequacy as a person		.34**		.09

* $p < .05$ level.
** $p < .01$ level.
*** $p < .001$ level.

these same 100 Q-sort characteristics and the 40-year WAIS IQs. This table shows that ten personality characteristics are correlated significantly with the 40-year IQs for both males and females. These characteristics include such aspects of intellectual functioning as: *appears to have a high degree of intellectual capacity; is verbally fluent, can express ideas well; is concerned with philosophical problems; able to see to the heart of important problems; genuinely values intellectual and cognitive matters; prides self on being objective, rational; has high aspiration level for self; is comfortable with uncertainty and complexities.* Two nonintellectual Q-sort items also correlated positively with high IQs at age 40: *Tends to feel guilty* and *does not arouse nurturant feelings in others.*

Highly significant sex differences emerged in this correlational analysis. Many of the girls' childhood characteristics, as judged by the case Q-sort of the first 18 years, correlated with their IQs at age 40. The reverse was true for the boys, where relatively few childhood but many 30-year characteristics were predictive. This may mean that personality-cognitive interaction occurs earlier in females than males, or that the occupational experiences of the men have evoked certain characteristics and cognitive-personality interrelationships. Among the characteristics of 30-year-olds that emerged as correlates of the men's (but not the women's) IQs at age 40 are: *is introspective; not responsive to humor; is not satisfied with his physical appearance; tends to ruminate and have persistent preoccupying thoughts; is not cheerful; does not handle anxiety and conflicts by repressive and dissociative tendencies.*

Women with high IQs at age 40 had the following characteristics during childhood (as judged by the 18-year case Q-sort): *is productive, gets things done; interprets basically simple situations in complicated ways; overconcerned with own adequacy as a person; enjoys esthetic impressions, is esthetically reactive.*

None of these characteristics, when rated at age 30 for women correlated significantly with their 40-year IQs. Characteristics rated at age 30, which did correlate with their 40-year IQs, are: *has a wide range of interests; does not create or exploit dependency.*

What can we make of these results? Those with high IQs are cognitively very able but tend to be self-critical, introspective, and not especially interested in other people; however, they are coping and highly thoughtful adults.

Thus far we have presented group results, but the greatest excitement lies in the individuals and in their "assimilation and accommodation" to life's experiences. We have selected six cases that show different patterns of intellectual growth. In looking at these cases we should keep in mind that, on the one hand, the correlations between the 6- and 40-year IQs are as high as .60; on the other hand, one-third of the group showed a variation of as much as 15 points of IQ at some time between 6 and 18 years.

Case 534 (see Figure. 2) illustrates a highly consistent performance from the age of 21 months to 40 years. Her scores at every age level were more than one standard deviation above the mean of the group. On her first test at 21 months, she kept asking for "more" games. At 3 years, she was judged "exceptionally bright." At later age levels, she was rated as shy, reserved, and self-conscious,

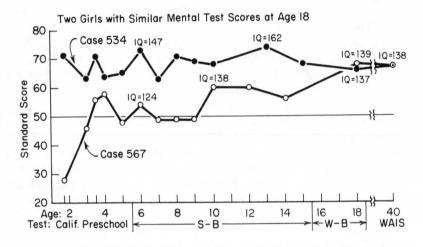

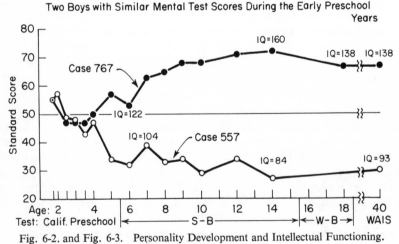

Fig. 6-2. and Fig. 6-3.   Personality Development and Intellectual Functioning.

but her attention and effort were excellent. She skipped one grade because "her social adjustment was not good and the work was too easy for her." Another teacher considered her poorly adjusted, brilliant, but difficult to work with. As a junior in high school, her teachers considered her reticent and shy but alert and conscientious. She has an A. B. degree, is married, and has four children whose IQs are all superior—but only one approaches her level of test performance. Both parents of this *S*, who are now in their 70's, were tested, and their IQs equaled her highly superior scores. Their WAIS EQs (or IQs not adjusted for the age decrement) would, of course, be lower.

Case 567's IQ at 18 is in line with the family's ability, but she did not do well on tests relative to the group in her early years. The testers mentioned her negativism, lack of effort, restlessness, and, at later ages, shyness; also, that "she turns in rather than out," and is unsure of herself. There were straining aspects of her home situation and probably chronic tension, but by the time she was in the 8th grade her teachers considered her a calm, happy, conscientious, thoughtful girl. She has an A. B. degree, is married, and her children are doing well academically.

Cases 767 and 557 (see Figure 3) obtained similar scores as preschool children, followed by a marked divergence in scores. The mature IQs of both men are in line with the family pattern, and the total of 12 children these men have fathered are earning IQs similar to those of their fathers—tempered by the IQs of their wives, which are nearer to the group average. Case 767, with his high IQ, has an A. B. degree and is in professional work. He earns a good salary, but so does Case 557, who is using his good mechanical skills and friendly ways to good advantage.

Case 767 in Figure 3 did not attain high IQs until well into elementary school, but we have two cases who were even slower in obtaining IQs that were in line with the family pattern. Case 531 (see Figure 4) is the architect described at the beginning of this paper. From the point of view of cognitive development, the most startling aspect of this record is the fact that at 18 years he did well on the Performance items of the Wechsler-Bellevue, which is predictive of later architectual interests, but it was not until the next test given at age 40 years that he excelled on Verbal subtests.

Case 562 (see Figure 4) was slow in achieving test scores that were in line with those of his parents, but his children are all earning superior scores as elementary and high school students. This man had a difficult time adjusting to parental demands and expectations as a child, and his slow gains in IQ may be reflecting his very difficult learning experiences.

In following, for 40 years, individual lives in process—with their great diversity of genetic constitution and associated temperament, rates of bio-

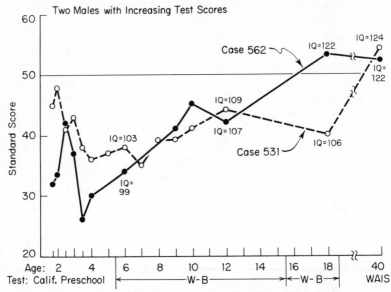

Fig. 6-4.   Personality Development and Intellectual Functioning.

logical growth, and varying environmental supports or strains diversely stimulating or inhibiting at different developmental stages—what general conclusions does one reach about personality and intelligence?

Briefly:

1.   The complexity of interacting factors is such that simplistic conclusions regarding any single factor, be it genetic or environmental, taken out of context of the other critically impinging factors, can easily add to ambiguous knowledge and poor predictions.

2.   No one really matures as a person or reaches his intellectual potential without an optimal amount of stress that forces more awareness—intrapersonal, interpersonal, and cognitive. Each individual, with his own unique combination of these many interacting facets, has to evolve for himself in his own style, and at his own speed, the coherent patterns that work for him.

3.   Intellectual and personal growth may go on, with new dimensions added over many decades—in contrast to the accepted "fact," when we began this study in 1928, that your IQ was your IQ and you had reached it by age 16!

4.   The intelligence scales did not include social intelligence, and some of

the very wise and perceptive Ss did not excel on the mental tests. In fact, some of the correlations reported in this paper suggest that the relation of "social intelligence" to the mental abilities measured by the Wechsler tests is extremely low.

In earlier studies of this group we have shown their increasing resemblance to the parental level of ability and that some individuals reach this level sooner than others (Honzik, 1957, 1963). We have shown that affectional relations among family members are related to later intellectual functioning, especially verbal abilities, but that the nature of the relevant affectional interactions differs for boys and girls (Honzik, 1967a and b). It is significant that gains in Verbal Ability continue during the adult years, when the impetus for superior language development usually occurs so early in life. We have noted quite remarkable similarities in both the total scores and profiles of abilities among the family members, which suggests the combined effect of both heredity and experience. Yakovlev (1960) reports that myelinization continues well beyond the midterm of the lifespan, suggesting that some gains may be a part of the genetic pattern; and we are very aware of the many experiences that are relevant to the development of intellectual functioning. While the statistical analyses made to date (the 40-year data are still being collected) of the personality variables are meager, they are relevant in that intellectual functioning, and maintenance of intellectual functioning, were found to be promoted and to reach the highest level in individuals who are not extreme in their masculinity or femininity, were not gregarious as children, but are, instead, introspective, intense, anxious, somewhat less social than average, and generally happier in the laboratory or study than in life's wider arena.

SUMMARY

Intellectual functioning was relatively stable over the age period 6 to 40 years for a representative urban sample. The average gain between 18 and 40 years on Wechsler tests was 3.8 IQ points. The only significant decline in score over this age period occurred on the Digit Symbol *speed* test. Ss who gained in IQ between 18 and 40 years were, as children, *not gregarious* or extreme in their *masculinity* or *femininity;* at age 30 they were *dissatisfied with their physical appearance* and were *not turned to for advice or reassurance.* Personality characteristics, observed in childhood and at age 30, which were related to high IQs at age 40, included *valuing intellectual matters,* a *high aspiration level,* and a *concern with philosophical problems.* These results suggest that individuals with high IQs in middle age were less social than average from an early age and were always interested in intellectual pursuits.

7 Educational Experience and the Maintenance of Intellectual Functioning by the Aged: An Overview

Samuel Granick and Alfred S. Friedman

Research on the intellectual functioning of the aged has documented quite forcefully an apparent pattern of general decline and deterioration. This has received considerable stress in the gerontological literature, with only very limited attention being given to the considerable residual capacities of the elderly and their potentials for effective performance and achievements. Even less attention seems to have been directed to the possibilities that the decline may not be as great as reported or even present in many instances. Rarely, of course, is there an indication that aging may be associated with growth or improved functioning in some areas.

The major proportion of research has, to a large extent, followed the orientation of our culture in focusing on the debilitating aspects of aging. It seems to have inadvertently helped to justify the tendency to view the aged as infirm and in constant need of support and protection. Associated with this are the powerful social, cultural, and economic pressures that lead the aged to disengage from active, dynamic involvement in society, and to withdraw into a depressed, deprived, and unproductive existence. To be old is tantamount to being shut out from communication with the things that count in the community and to be an object of pity and condescension. It is hardly surprising to find the widespread sense of reluctance on the part of people to admit to being old. Alternatively, those who call themselves old reflect a sense of resignation and sadness about their circumstances, perceiving themselves as impotent and presenting an exaggerated picture of their incapacity and lack of usefulness.

Evidence is accumulating, however, which may serve as a basis for modifying this picture along more optimistic lines. Lorge (1955) and others called attention quite a few years ago to the possible relationship between the evident extensive intellectual decline of the aged and their relatively low educational status. Birren and Morrison (1961) analyzed the WAIS standardization data for the possible effects of the negative correlation of age with education on the scores of the various age groups. They found that education was a very important feature of the "general intellective component," derived by the Hotelling principal component method. When the scores on the subtests were statistically adjusted for this factor, relatively little decline with age was found in the sample of Subjects (Ss). Granick and Friedman (1967) used the partial correlation technique along similar lines with a group of non-institutional, psychiatrically normal older adults, to whom a battery of 33 verbal, perceptual, cognitive, and psychomotor tests had been administered. When education was partialed out, the number of tests showing significant decline with age was reduced from 27 to 19 (a 30 per cent decrease), with mainly the measures of "sensory efficiency, psychomotor speed, perceptual flexibility, and abstract thinking" continuing to show decline with age. These findings appear related to the results of the longitudinal studies of well-educated adults of above-average intelligence by Bayley and Oden (1955) and by Owens (1966), who reported no decline on some tests of intellectual abilities and relatively little decline on others. Also supporting the principle of a negative relationship between education and rate of intellectual decline is the review, by Welford (1958), of research on learning and performance skills in the aged. Studies are cited to provide evidence along this line with respect to such cognitive functions as the use of ingenuity in problem-solving, learning an artificial language, completing number series, solving arithmetic problems, recalling a prose passage, understanding analogies, and drawing logical inferences.

A number of other investigations have been reported, both of a longitudinal character (Granick and Birren, 1969; Jarvik and Falek, 1963), as well as of the cross-sectional type (Granick and Friedman, 1966; Schaie and Strother, 1968), which clearly demonstrate that older adults, even of advanced age—in their seventies and eighties—can perform quite effectively on tests of intellectual functioning. Factors of physical health and morale are found to be important in enabling the Ss to demonstrate and use their abilities. Those who are free of disease, especially of the cardiovascular types, and who are adequately stimulated socially and emotionally, perform as well as younger adults, particularly on verbal materials and also where speed of response and motor coordination are not involved (Botwinick and Birren, 1963; Granick and Birren, 1969).

Learning and memory experiments have also appeared which modify considerably the traditionally negative picture of the aged individual's capacities for acquiring new information and skills. Lorge (1955) was among the early investigators who called attention to the likelihood that elderly Ss could learn as well as younger age groups when the factor of speed is eliminated with respect to stimulus presentation and response requirements. He also put stress on evidence suggesting that the quality of the learning of the elderly compared favorably with that of young adults. Fairly recent work by Canestrari (1963), Arenberg (1965), and Eisdorfer (1965) supports the hypothesis that the aged show decreased deficit in learning ability when such noncognitive factors as speed and anxiety are reduced or eliminated. Their Ss did not learn as well as younger age groups, but the quality of their performance increased significantly. The earlier noted good-quality intellectual functioning on verbal intelligence tests by healthy senescent Ss who are highly motivated is matched by comparable results in learning experiments (Botwinick and Birren, 1963).

It seems clear that the aged have considerable intellectual potential and ability to learn and benefit from education. The well-known productivity, high-level mental functioning, and creative output of many elderly individuals who remain active and involved in new learning experiences suggest that educational stimulation may accomplish this for many others. Almost certainly, however, we may anticipate, on the basis of available evidence, that education can play a significant role in enabling the aged to maintain their intellectual effectiveness.

Interest in learning tends to increase in all adult age groups, including the elderly, in direct relation to their educational attainments (Johnstone and Rivera, 1965). This interest is matched by the fact that the rate of participation in adult education activities is also related to the previously acquired level of education. Accordingly, it appears that those who already have a good deal of education and exposure to learning are the most likely to continue adding to their knowledge and to maintain their intellectual effectiveness. This tendency augurs well for the future, since census data have shown a continuous rise in educational level for succeeding age groups. Thus, a projection to 1985 of the educational status of the U. S. population (U. S. Bureau of the Census, 1965) indicates that 61 per cent of persons 65 years and over will then have had a high school education or better.

The educational level of the current population of elderly, however, is far less favorable: about one-fifth of those over 65 years have four years or less of schooling and only about one-third have gone beyond the eighth grade (U.S. Bureau of the Census, 1960). This restricted educational experience appears related to the very limited use that people over age 55 (about 10 per cent compared to about 30 per cent of those under age 35) seem to be making of available adult education activities (Johnstone and Rivera, 1965). A census report on enrollment in adult education classes (U. S. Bureau of the Census, 1958) is even more pessimistic for the aged, showing only 2.8 per cent of 60- to 74-year-olds and 1.1 per cent of those 75 years and over participating in such classes.

Considerable awareness of this unhappy situation is shown by writers on the subject of education for the elderly. It is noted that educational opportunities for adults of all ages are fairly abundant and that the elderly take relatively little advantage of what is available (Donahue, 1956; Webber, 1963). It appears as though they have very limited motivation to further their cultural development and the maintenance of their intellectual capabilities. Webber (1963) suggests that essentially the aged may be acting in terms of social expectations, since society seems to assign few or only limited specific constructive functions to the elderly, a situation unlike that existing for children and younger adults. Moreover, there are few educational opportunities, as noted by Pressey (1956), which are adapted to the needs and circumstances of the aged. Thus, even those who may be inclined to seek means of furthering their intellectual status are very often frustrated by such obstacles as awkward physical arrangements, inappropriate time schedules, and uncomfortable social settings. These factors, along with their reduced physical energy level, contribute to the poor motivation shown by the vast majority of the aged for education of both the formal and informal varieties.

Perhaps the most important element to be considered in the education of the aged is the matter of goals. Pablo Casals is quoted as responding to the question as to why he still practices several hours each day, with the remark that it is "because I think I am improving." Thus, even though the desire to learn tends to decline with age, there is evidence that interest in learning new things is shown by both old and young people when they can look forward to some kind of practical outcome, such as higher income, occupational advancement, or geographic mobility (Johnstone and Rivera, 1965).

It seems self-evident that education acts as a stimulus to the individual's capabilities and that the exercise of these capabilities is likely to maintain, and even increase, their functional effectiveness. Conversely, the failure to use one's intellectual capacities on a regular and extensive basis may lead to a sort of intellectual atrophy and to rapid deterioration of the ability to perform even fairly elementary mental tasks. Research workers, as may be evident from the above review, have been slow in providing a scientific basis for these two propositions with respect to the aged, but studies in child development do provide ample support. Those interested in the practical, programming aspects of the situation, on the other hand, have not been slow to come forth with forceful statements on the need to provide educational facilities, stimulation, and direct help for the aged to enable them to maintain and even improve their intellectual functioning. Some of the proposed ideas that appear challenging and promising are:

1.   Education should be organized for the total life cycle; for the aged, it should be related to their practical needs and goals.

2.   Education for retirement should start early so that a person will have a basis for selecting and defining specific goals for himself as he advances in years.

3.   Education for retirement should involve helping individuals to define and select new social roles for themselves as they move into later maturity. Included here is education of the public toward perceiving aging in more positive terms and toward providing the aged with broader social and economic opportunities than is currently the case.

4.   Educational programming should include participation of the aged in both the planning and execution of whatever projects may be developed.

5.   Energy and funds should be expended for the development of prosthetic devices and special learning programs or procedures to enable the aged to compensate for their handicaps and thus improve their functional effectiveness.

SUMMARY

In general, current writers on the subject reflect a tone of optimism about education for the aged and its potentially positive effects on their intellectual and social functioning. They point to the increased concern of the government, business organizations, educational facilities, communications media, and community health and welfare agencies. The aged are themselves becoming assertive and are playing an active role in producing the necessary changes in their own and the public's attitudes. We are inclined to be confident in predicting that the recent White House Conference on Aging will focus quite extensively and forcefully on education for the aged with a view to providing and developing means for making the latter part of the life cycle a more effective, productive, and satisfying period of life than has been the case to date.

8 Discussion: Patterns of Intellectual Functioning in the Later Years

Lissy F. Jarvik

The preceding chapters, which described the major longitudinal research on intellectual changes with advancing age, have given us a preview of the results we may expect from these and similar studies.

Despite differences in the composition of the samples with regard to age, intelligence, education, socioeconomic background, and other relevant variables, there appears to be at least one common thread leading toward a cohesive pattern of intellectual functioning in the later years of life.

That thread seems to be the remarkable stability of verbal scores—whenever health has been preserved—accompanied by a relentlessly progressive decline in performance on speeded tasks. Thus, our longitudinal studies have led us to rediscover the classical pattern of aging! And this pattern is evident under a wide variety of circumstances. As described a decade ago by Eisdorfer, Busse, and Cohen (1959), the dissociation of cognitive stability from psychomotor deterioration occurred regardless of age group (between the ages of 60 and 75 years), irrespective of intelligence level (high or low), and without reference either to socioeconomic status (two levels were investigated) or to residential setting (mental hospital or community). The classical pattern was seen in all of the subgroups. As a matter of fact, we can now extend the range below 60, since Drs. Honzik and Macfarlane (Chapter 6) reported that decline on speeded motor tasks begins between the ages of 18 and 40 years, at a time when verbal scores are still increasing. Although Eichorn's data (Chapter 1) tended to show gains between the ages of 16 and 36 years in performance as well as in verbal scores, the greatest and most consistent gains apparently occurred in a verbal test—Vocabulary.

Even if we look at the *total* instead of the subtest scores, as Drs. Eisdorfer and Wilkie (Chapter 4), Rhudick and Gordon (Chapter 2), and Schoenfeldt (Chapter 5) have done, *the stability of intellectual abilities emerges once more.* From Dr. Schoenfeldt's report, we learn that the Iowa subjects, who were entering the seventh decade at the time of their last testing, had maintained their relative standings on mean total Alpha scores for 42 years. Eisdorfer and Wilkie, and Rhudick and Gordon, whose subjects were followed from the seventh to the eighth decades, were also impressed by their failure to find rapid declines in these later years.

However, as pointed out by Drs. Granick and Friedman (Chapter 7), the level of education is a cogent factor in intellectual functioning during later life. Undoubtedly, as they observe, education serves to stimulate intellectual interests and helps to set up habit patterns that perpetuate such interests throughout the life span. But more may be involved: as Drs. Honzik and Macfarlane note, it is the personality features which often determine whether intellectual pursuits are undertaken or not, and may even identify those who decline in intellectual functioning provided the preliminary findings of Drs. Rhudick and Gordon are confirmed.

From Dr. Blum and colleagues, we may deduce that the natural course of aging in man does *not* include cognitive decline. This conclusion is not a novel one, but was already stated by Dr. Birren (1970, p. 125) as follows:

> "There is the possibility that the psychological norm for the species is one of little change in intellectual function in the years after 65, given good health."

That health status is a key factor has emerged from Dr. Birren's studies, from data obtained by Palmore (1969), Riegel (1969), Schaie (Personal Communication), and now also from the Wilkie-Eisdorfer longitudinal data presented in Chapter 10. Apparently, vascular diseases exert a potent destructive influence upon intellectual functioning, and it is the effect of such vascular disease that is most likely responsible for the relationship between *cognitive decline and mortality* observed by those of us engaged in longitudinal research.

From our own research at the New York State Psychiatric Institute, if illness does *not* intervene, cognitive stability is the rule and can be maintained into the ninth decade, as shown by one of our twins who was tested five times between the ages of 62 and 82 years. At age 82 this lady scored higher than she had at age 62 on Vocabulary, Similarities, and Digits Backward, and she equaled her earlier performance on Digits Forward. Only on the speeded motor tasks were there prominent decrements. If deviations from the classical pattern are taken as clues to underlying pathology, they may lead to prompt diagnosis prior to the appearance of gross symptomatology.

We can go even further and ask whether the precipitous psychomotor decline has to be accepted as inevitable. Probably not! We know that there are wide individual differences, and our 82-year-old lady had shown less than a 1 per cent annual decline on Tapping and Digit Symbol Substitution. She is clearly an exceptional person, however, and the general aging pattern remains one of marked decline in speeded tasks.

This decline is a particular handicap in a culture where the emphasis is on speed and rapid acquisition of new knowledge, as is the case in North America today. We would do well to remember that the *incompetence* of senior citizens stressed in our own society stands in sharp contrast to the *wisdom* of the aged revered in many other cultures. In *focusing* on total intelligence, we have too long ignored that there may be some truth after all in Cicero's statement that "intelligence, reflection, and judgment reside in the old."

With the foregoing chapters, we have at last returned to pose the right question. We have made a turnabout from the usual quest for information on age-correlated *deterioration* and looked instead at the factors associated with the *maintenance* of intellectual functioning in the later years of life.

Part II
Somatic Components
of Psychological Changes
in Adults

9 Mechanisms of Brain-
Body Interaction in
the Aged

William G. Troyer

Other contributors (Chapters 10, 11, and 12) have demonstrated that changes in motor, cognitive, and brain electrical behavior are correlated with changes in heart rate and blood pressure in the aging organism. It is tempting to analyze the sequence of these changes to determine if the changes in the central nervous system (CNS) are related causally or consequentially to the cardiovascular events, or are independent of them. Before attempting such an analysis, let us consider some historical contributions and some of the structural and functional aspects of the problem.

HISTORICAL CONTRIBUTIONS

René Descartes is credited, or blamed, for the philosophic separation of body and mind. The historical belief in the disconnection of the viscera from the brain probably stems from the Cartesian influence on modern scientific thought. Others, particularly writers, who were not so inclined to be tied to dogma, provided anecdotes to the contrary. Charles Dickens recounts the death of Anthony Chuzzlewit and the faint of Miss Pecksniff, both of which were stimulated by discovering that people they loved did not reciprocate their feelings. More recently, brain stimulation studies by Hess (1957) and many others have demonstrated that the CNS can modify visceral activity (Rushmer and Smith, 1959). Harold Wolff and his co-workers (1968) have extended these findings to patients with many diseases. Wolff's usual experimental paradigm consisted of stress and neutral interviews with patients while measuring a physiological response related to the pathogenesis of the disease. For instance, the diastolic blood pressure of a 30-year-old unmarried woman increased 25 mm of mercury (Hg) during a discussion of her hostile relationship with her mother (Wolff, et al. 1955).

While these experiments demonstrate unequivocally that the CNS may modify peripheral functions, they do not eliminate the possibility that altered visceral activity may modify behavior that traditionally has been considered of entirely central origin. The patient with an illness of a visceral organ frequently does not "feel well" before the onset of more specific symptoms, and some observers have speculated that visceral disease processes may manifest themselves as changes in affects and dreams long before they become evident in a more traditional clinical manner (Giovacchini and Muslim, 1965; Mirsky, 1959). Further, Lange and James (1922) long ago suggested that peripheral musculoskeletal and visceral events were important determinants of emotions. Hohmann investigated the relationship between the level of transection of the spinal cord and reported emotional feelings; he found that the greater the disruption of the spinal cord, the greater the decrease in some emotional experiences (Hohmann, 1966). Two possibilities exist to explain this as well as related phenomena. The brain may be receiving information from the viscera, and/or a central process may control both the state of the organ and behavior.

CURRENT CONCEPTS

The work of Thompson and Nowlin provides an important clue to the sequence of events taking place (Chapter 12). They demonstrated that peripheral visceral events (cardiac slowing), as well as central events (cortical negativity), occurred during a simple motor behavioral task (reaction time to a light). In young subjects (Ss), cardiac slowing and an increase in cortical negativity occurred during the foreperiod of the reaction time trials. The speed of reaction time was correlated with the magnitude of the cardiac slowing. In aged Ss the reaction time was longer and cardiac slowing was less. There was no detectable difference in the change in cortical negativity between old and young. These data suggest that the speed of motor reaction time is determined more by what occurred peripherally than centrally. Indeed, Lacey (1967) has proposed that peripheral autonomic events assist in the regulation of central nervous system arousal via visceral afferent receptors. Obrist et al. (1970) have recently challenged Lacey's hypothesis with an experiment that showed no difference in reaction times when cardiac slowing was abolished by the use of drugs. He interprets the data to mean that cardiac deceleration is not a primary link in the attention process during the reaction time task.

Further analysis of this interpretation of Thompson and Nowlin's data leads one to ask why less cardiac slowing occurs in the aged than in the young. Are central and peripheral events slowed down gradually? If so, why is cortical negativity unchanged? Is this measure not as sensitive an indicator of central events as reaction time, or does the answer lie outside the CNS? Are the information pathways to and from the CNS slower in the old than in the young? Is the conduction system of the heart capable of responding to cardiac deceleration signals if they are transmitted from the CNS in the aged? And if cardiac slowing is essential for a fast reaction time, how does the information get from the heart to the finger?

These questions are really part of a larger question. What are the ways in which the brain is connected to the rest of the organism? A neurophysiologist would ask the question in terms of brain inputs and outputs. What are the mechanisms by which the brain receives, integrates, and transmits information to and from the other structures of the body?

The CNS receives information from two sources. Information from the external environment is received from visual, auditory, tactile, olfactory, and taste stimuli. The internal environment is monitored by humoral and neural mechanisms. Specific areas in subcortical structures have been identified which are sensitive to the concentration of substances transported in the blood. Glucose, sodium, sex hormones, and adrenal hormones modify such subcortical receptor sites. The information received is integrated, and appropriate behavioral and visceral responses are initiated. In the case of an increased concentration of sodium in the blood, urine output is decreased and drinking behavior is increased. The effects of aging on such receptor areas have not been systematically studied, although endocrine and metabolic systems such as glucose tolerance are known to change with age (Gitman, 1967).

Humoral agents may transmit information about specific regions of the internal environment. For example, the blood level of thyroid hormone provides some indication of the activity of the thyroid gland even though it does not distinguish various regions within the gland. Clearly the rapidity with which humorally conducted messages are supplied to the CNS is dependent upon the velocity of blood flow. Apparently, the more specific the information, the more rapidly it is carried to the CNS and the faster output commands are performed.

The rest of this discussion will focus on the structure and function of the autonomic efferent and visceral afferent systems—first in general and then in the aged organism.

STRUCTURE AND FUNCTION OF THE VISCERAL NERVOUS SYSTEM (VNS)

All visceral structures and blood vessels are innervated by nerve fibers, the cell bodies of which originate in the brain stem, spinal cord, paravertebral, and visceral ganglia. Innervated structures contain receptors that respond to transmitter substance released by the nerve endings, as well as other receptors that respond to the state of the innervated structure. Structures which transmit information from the CNS to the periphery are called efferent nerve fibers. Those which transmit information in the opposite direction are called afferent nerve fibers. Another way of classifying autonomic nerves is based on the difference in the neurotransmitter liberated at the nerve ending in response to a stimulus. Those liberating acetylcholine are called parasympathetic; those releasing norepinephrine are called sympathetic. In addition to the neurotransmitters liberated by nerve endings, the adrenal medulla releases epinephrine (adrenalin) and norepinephrine (noradrenalin) into the bloodstream, which can also stimulate efferent and afferent structures. The writer has chosen the name visceral nervous system (VNS) because the term "autonomic nervous system" is no longer true in light of recent successes in conditioning a wide variety of visceral responses and it does not include the afferent pathways. As Miller has pointed out, the autonomic nervous system has been regarded traditionally as independent of voluntary control. This is no longer thought to be true since he and his collaborators have succeeded in conditioning a wide variety of visceral responses to external stimuli in small animals (Miller, 1969). Engel and his colleagues have demonstrated voluntary control of heart rate in humans (Engel and Hansen, 1966; Levene et al. 1968).

RECEPTORS AND REFLEXES

The effect of the neurotransmitter on target tissue is determined not only by the type and quantity of neurotransmitter released, but by the type and quantity of receptors activated. Acetylcholine activates receptors that produce slow heart rates (bradycardia), peripheral vasodilation, and contraction of visceral smooth muscle. Norepinephrine and epinephrine, both catecholamines, are compounds that are closely related in chemical structure and function. Two receptors, known as alpha and beta, seem to account for most of their actions. Beta receptors produce relaxation of smooth muscle in blood vessels, bronchi, and other structures; they mediate the mobilization of free fatty acids from adipose tissue, increase the force of contraction of cardiac muscle, and accelerate heart rate. Alpha receptors produce constriction of smooth muscle in blood vessels and bronchi—actions that are antagonistic to beta receptors. No alpha receptors have been found in the heart or adipose tissue. The mechanisms determining which receptor a molecule of catecholamine will activate in a tissue with both receptors, such as a blood vessel, are not clear.

In contrast to the extensive data known about effector receptors that respond to transmitter substances, intensive investigation of receptors that respond to the metabolic and physiological state of the tissue is just beginning. Adám (1967) and Paintal (1963) have reviewed these recently. The first afferent visceral receptors (interoceptors) observed were stretch receptors in the aortic arch and in the sinus of the carotid artery. When blood pressure increased in these areas, decreased heart rate and peripheral vasodilatation are observed. The afferent impulses produced by the baroreceptors are carried over branches of the glossopharyngeal and vagus nerves to the brain stem, where contact is made with the efferent arm of the reflex. This reflex constitutes a feedback loop for the control of systemic blood pressure because a decrease in heart rate and an increase in the size of peripheral arterioles result in a decrease in blood pressure and hence fewer afferent impulses to the brain stem. This reflex has been used recently for the treatment of systemic hypertension and severe angina pectoris (Braunwald et al., 1967).

Braunwald and his co-workers have implanted a small radio-controlled pulse generator connected to platinum electrodes on the nerve from the carotid sinus of patients with angina pectoris. By activating the radio transmitter, the patient can stimulate this nerve and produce a decrease in heart rate and peripheral vascular resistance. The decrease in heart rate and peripheral vascular resistance lowers the oxygen requirements of the heart, which in turn relieves the symptoms of angina.

In addition to the receptors which regulate systemic blood pressure, there appear to be local baroreceptors which may play a role in regulating blood flow to specific glands. Niijima and Winter (1968) have recently described afferent nerve fibers from the adrenal medulla which respond specifically to local blood pressure fluctuations.

Another important category of afferent receptors are the chemoreceptors. The best-known of these is located in the carotid sinus and responds to changes in the concentration of arterial carbon dioxide. More recently, Winter and Niijima have suggested that epinephrine-sensitive receptors are present in the adrenal medulla, and Niijima has demonstrated a glucose-sensitive receptor in the liver (Niijima, 1969; Winter and Niijima, 1968).

FUNCTION OF VISCERAL EFFERENT AND AFFERENT NERVOUS SYSTEMS

Before considering the effects of the aging process on the VNS, it is first necessary to consider normal physiological functions. Certain phylogenetic observations are useful. Norepinephrine and epinephrine do not appear to act as neurotransmitters in animals lower than vertebrates (Prosser, 1959). Chromaffin tissue, the analogue of the adrenal medulla, appears in early vertebrates but does not become organized as the adrenal medulla until mammals (Hartman and Brownell, 1949). Relatively simple organisms, such as sponges, have a nervous system composed of a network of short fibers. More complex organisms possess nervous systems of long nerve fibers of various sizes. Thus, large fibers, with norepinephrine as a neurotransmitter, and the adrenal medulla are late additions to the neural apparatus when measured in terms of evolutionary processes. Winter and Niijima (1968) have speculated—on the basis of the work of Parker, Bishop, and Grundfest— that fiber size increases as the organism becomes more independent of its environment. If this is indeed the case, then tonic (small) fibers might function to maintain the tone of an organ, whereas phasic (large) fibers would transmit impulses necessary for moment-to-moment adaptation. We have already seen that certain receptors regulate systemic blood pressure, while others in the adrenal medulla seem to be responsive to local changes in pressure. This suggests there may be local feedback loops for vascular pressure regulation in addition to systemic reflexes. It is also probable that neural receptors at both local and central levels of organization exist for such substances as glucose, hormones, and other compounds.

The visceral nervous system develops during fetal life, but is incomplete at birth. Further development of the sympathetic portion, and perhaps fetal development as well, seem to be under control of a specific nerve growth-promoting factor (Levi-Montalcini and Angeletti, 1968). When antibodies to this factor are given to newborn animals, further development of the sympathetic nervous system is impaired, a procedure known as immunosympathectomy. Animals who have been immunosympathectomized have been shown to be more susceptible to cold environments than animals with an intact sympathetic nervous system, and demonstrate some differences in behavior in classical conditioning experiments (Fehr, 1966). The mechanisms regulating nerve growth-promoting factor are unknown. Since other protein hormones have been shown to be regulated by the central nervous system, it is tempting to speculate that early infantile experiences might influence this substance and hence subsequent development of the sympathetic nervous system.

Walter Cannon (1953) and his colleagues carried out a series of experiments in the early half of the century on what was known then as the autonomic nervous system and found changes that were produced by a wide variety of physical and psychological stimuli. They concluded that the sympathetic nervous system responded *en masse*. Experiments since that time suggest that this is not necessarily so and that significant specificity of action occurs. For example, when the head is immersed in water while diving, reflex vasoconstriction of all blood vessels except to the brain and heart occurs, a sympathetic response, and at the same time the heart rate slows, a parasympathetic response (Scholander, 1961–62). The work of Miller and his colleagues has demonstrated even greater specificity by the use of operant conditioning techniques (Miller, 1969). They have been able to condition independently increases or decreases of heart rate, blood pressure, gastrointestinal motility, urine flow, and vasomotor tone in acute animal experiments. These experiments and techniques have considerable theoretical and practical implications. The very fact that conditioning occurred implies that the efferent arm of the visceral nervous system is not automatic, that it learns to discriminate, and that it can be brought under a certain amount of voluntary control. Weiss and Engel (in 1971) have used these techniques to treat patients with irregularities of cardiac rate and rhythm who have been refractory to drug therapy, and Lang and Melamed (1969) have successfully treated an infant with chronic recurrent vomiting.

Discrimination has been shown to take place in the afferent arm of the visceral nervous system. Ádám (1967) has demonstrated that interoceptive stimuli can be used as a conditioned stimulus in a classical conditioning paradigm and as a contingency in an operant conditioning paradigm. Further, he has demonstrated considerable topographical specificity of visceral afferents. For instance, balloon expansion in the ureter has been used as an unconditioned response and can produce a conditioned response (CR) on the electroencephalogram. When balloon pressure is applied to a point 5 centimeters inferiorly from the original point where conditioning occurred, the CR is no longer elicited.

Ádám has also provided data to support the Lacey hypothesis that visceral afferents are important mediators of exteroceptive learning. He conditioned three groups of rats to press a lever for food in response to a reinforced contingency. Bilateral carotid sinus denervation was performed in one group (A), and unilateral in another (B); the third was left intact (C). The latencies of group A were shortest, those of C were the longest, and those of B were in the middle. These data would suggest that an intact carotid sinus inhibits performance.

However, when the animals were presented a task in which they were required to discriminate between the reinforced contingency and a similar but unreinforced contingency, the group with intact carotid sinuses performed best, those with bilateral denervation performed worst, and those with unilateral denervation were intermediate. Thus it appears that the carotid sinus functions to inhibit performance, and this function is particularly useful in a learning situation.

One method of studying the function of the visceral nervous system is to investigate the experiments of nature in which one of its activities has been decreased or increased. One of these instances is a disease known as familial dysautonomia, which occurs early in life in Jewish families (32). Prominent among the symptoms are absence of tears, postural hypotension, dysphagia, and "crises" of vomiting, hypertension, cutaneous blotching, and sweating often induced by emotional stress. Other findings include an absence of tongue taste-bud papillae and a relative insensitivity to pain. Death usually occurs in childhood, but some affected persons live into the third decade. Analysis of the catecholamine content of cardiac and adrenal medullary tissue reveal increased levels (33). These data plus the defects in sensation suggest that the fundamental cause of this disease may be an inability to detect, transmit, or integrate afferent information.

Norepinephrine and epinephrine producing tumors of the adrenal medulla and other chromaffin tissue are frequently found in man. The most prominent symptom complex associated with these tumors is hypertension, headaches, sweating, tremor, and anxiety attacks. A form of myocarditis and heart failure may occur. After removal of the tumor by surgery, which can often be quite hazardous, the patient is usually without evidence of serious side effects from prolonged exposure to high levels of catecholamines. It should be remembered that circulating catecholamines do not mimic accurately all the functions of catecholamine released from sympathetic nerve endings (34). In other words, excess circulating catecholamines whether from pheochromocytomas or exogenously administered catecholamines, the latter a familiar technique used in the investigation of the effects of the sympathetic nervous system, do not always accurately mimic the effects of sympathetic nerve stimulation.

In contrast to excess levels of catecholamines, surgical removal of the adrenal medulla and sympathetic ganglia results in decreased levels of catecholamines. This procedure has been used for many years in the treatment of systemic hypertention. In addition to the expected changes in blood pressure and sweat gland regulation Whitelaw and Smithwick found marked changes in sexual function, particularly in obtaining erection and ejaculation (35). More recently, drugs which block the sympathetic nervous system have taken the place of surgical sympathectomy. The same kinds of effects on sexual function are frequently observed.

Organ transplantation offers an opportunity for studying the function of visceral nerves since a transplanted organ has its nerve supply severed. This denervation is not permanent and not complete. Sympathetic postganglionic and parasympathetic preganglionic fibers slowly regenerate. This process takes approximately one year in the surgically denervated dog heart. The parasympathetic postganglionic fibers remain intact because only the preganglionic fibers are severed by the surgical procedure.

One difficulty in interpreting data from transplant studies in that the organ may still respond to circulating neurotransmitters. In fact, its response may be exaggerated in the case of epinephrine or norepinephrine because the sympathetic nerves no longer inactivate the neurotransmitter by metabolic or reuptake mechanisms. This state of an exaggerated response, known as denervation hypersensitivity, also applies to parasympathetically innervated areas when acetylcholine is applied to a denervated area.

Data from human studies are scant because few heart transplant recipients have survived and many factors that are difficult to control can affect the results. More patients with kidney transplants have survived and the donor makes an ideal control for the study of neural influence on the kidney. However, the functions of the nerves innervating the kidney are either unknown; no suitable procedure for evaluating function in the intact human exists; or the studies have been performed after some nerve regeneration might be expected to have occurred. Little has been learned, from the use of this model, about the neural influence on the kidney.

Cardiac denervation and transplantation has been studied extensively in dogs. In the immediate postoperative period, these animals develop heart failure and must be maintained on digitalis. After recovery from surgery, the resting heart rates are increased and not affected by respiration. When exercised, the animals show a slower rate of rise of heart rate than intact animals, but eventually achieve an equal level. The slowness of the response is due to humoral transport of catecholamines rather than to a direct release of the same neurotransmitter by an intact fiber. When drugs which block the effects of circulating epinephrine on the heart are given, the animal's exercise tolerance is markedly diminished.

In summary, many functions of the visceral nerves are known. Data from disease processes, transplants, and surgical and pharmacological denervation studies indicate that an intact visceral nervous system is necessary for the important biological functions of reproduction, upright posture, and locomotion. In the cardiovascular system it is particularly concerned with the speed with which changes occur in heart rate and vascular tone. Its role in the mediation of other forms of behavior needs to be studied much further.

FINDINGS IN THE AGING ORGANISM

Evidence for the effects of the aging process on the visceral nervous system comes from three sources. First, certain psychological functions that have parasympathetic and sympathetic correlates change with age, and the neural components also change. Second, much data on physiological parameters, at least in part regulated by the visceral nervous system, have been obtained. Few data have been obtained on the changes of these parameters when the visceral component has been blocked. Third, a few studies of direct visceral function in aging have been performed.

Many studies have shown changes in psychological function associated with age; these have been recently reviewed by Eisdorfer (1967), who has studied verbal learning changes in aging. Eisdorfer's work has demonstrated that verbal serial rote learning in the aged S (over 60) is significantly diminished when the duration of the stimulus exposure interval is four seconds but not when it is ten seconds. Further, he has shown that differential changes in neural activity accompany the changes in verbal behavior. Most recently, Eisdorfer, Nowlin, and Wilkie (1970) have used a pharmacological agent to block the sympathetic influences on heart rate and other arousal responses in a group of aged subjects performing a verbal learning task. A significant increment in learning was observed in those subjects whose sympathetic nervous system was blocked.

Three implications can be drawn from this work: (1) neural activity accompanies verbal learning; (2) changes in neural activity are reflected in changes in verbal behavior; and (3) changes in verbal learning ability in the old person are significantly different from the young only when the stimulus exposure time is shortened. Many of the differences attributed to the aging process might be accounted for on the basis of temporal differences. We shall attempt to understand the structural basis for this finding.

The VNS contributes to many physiological processes. A good example is the cardiovascular system, in which heart rate, strength of contraction of the heart, and size of peripheral blood vessels are partially regulated by the VNS. The effect of age on heart rate has been extensively studied (Mithoefer and Karetzky, 1968). Resting heart rate decreases with age. With exercise at constant oxygen consumption levels, peak heart rate is lower in the aged and the post-exercise return to normal is prolonged (Norris et al., 1953). Modern Western investigators have not examined the neural components of these changes, but Russian investigators have been active in this field.

Frolkis (1966) injected atropine, a drug that blocks the effect of the parasympathetic nerves on heart rate, into young adults and old people and found a significantly greater increase in heart rate in the young. In order to block the sympathetic effects on the heart he injected dihydroergotamine into the same Ss and found a greater decrease in heart rate in the young than in the old. These data suggest that there is a decrease in both sympathetic and parasympathetic influences on the resting heart rate of the aged. In order to further localize the origin of these changes, Frolkis performed a series of experiments on sympathetic, parasympathetic, and visceral afferent nerves, ganglia, afferent and efferent receptors, and brain nerve centers in small animals.

He demonstrated that smaller amounts of neurotransmitter, applied directly to the target organ, were required to obtain the same effect in the aged animal as in the young. In old cats, contraction of the nictitating membrane occurred with the administration of 2.7 μgm/kg of norepinephrine or 0.2 μgm/kg of epinephrine, whereas the two- to three-year-old cats required 26.2 μgm/kg of norepinephrine or 1.9 μgm/kg of epinephrine for the same effect. Acetylcholine sensitivity was tested on a preparation of skeletal muscle. Contraction of skeletal muscle was obtained with 5.8 μgm/kg of acetylcholine in old rabbits and 13.5 μgm/kg in young rabbits.

Frolkis next examined the thresholds of visceral efferent nerves to electrical stimulation. These were found to be increased in old animals as compared to young ones. In 10- to 12-month-old rats the excitation threshold of the vagus nerve, as indicated by bradycardia, was 0.52 volts (v), and in 28- to 32-month-old rats it was 1.15 v. Sympathetic nerve thresholds, as indicated by contraction of the nictitating membrane, required 42 per cent greater stimulation in the old than in the young. These thresholds were obtained by observing a functional response. Since the target organ is already more sensitive to neurotransmitter, fewer units of neurotransmitter were probably released by the stimulation in the old than in the young. If the number of molecules of neurotransmitter released, rather than the functional response, were to be used as a criterion, the nerve stimulation thresholds in the old would be even higher. The use of voltage as an indication of thresholds in peripheral nerves deserves a word of caution. Significant changes in the quality and magnitude of tissue water and electrolytes undoubtedly occur during the aging process. These factors affect voltage and current as well; the amount of current delivered to the nerve is the important variable, and apparatus is available to insure that a constant current is delivered during nerve stimulation.

Frolkis next examined the excitability of ganglia and the effects of various stimuli on central nerve centers. The excitability, determined by electrical stimulation, of the upper cervical ganglion decreased with age. The sensitivity to acetylcholine and ganglionic blocking agents was increased in the ganglion and decreased in the nerve centers. These data are consistent with those obtained from peripheral receptors. The effects of stimulants on central nerve centers demonstrated more sensitivity in the old than in the young. However, methodological details which might convince one that this finding is not mediated by a peripheral mechanism are lacking.

On the efferent side Frolkis summarizes his findings by suggesting that the tissues of aged persons are less sensitive to neural influences, but more sensitive to the same neurotransmitter contained by the same nerve fibers. In more conventional terms, his findings might be interpreted as indicative of a state of partial denervation hypersensitivity. Denervation hypersensitivity occurs when either acetylcholine- or noradrenalin-containing fibers are destroyed. The effector organ has a greater response to a given amount of respective neurotransmitter. In the adrenergic system this occurs because the reuptake mechanism is no longer producing physiological inactivation. Partial support for this interpretation comes from additional data of Frolkis', showing decreases in the tissue levels of cholinesterase and acetylcholine associated with age.

Two related questions are raised by the hypothesis of *denervation* hypersensitivity. What experiments could be done to support it, and what size fibers are lost preferentially? Botár (1966) has demonstrated a loss of visceral nerve fibers, neurons, and ganglia associated with age. Further, his data demonstrate a preferential loss of small fibers, but his techniques do not distinguish between efferent and afferent fibers. Other studies that would provide additional data would include age-related changes in tissue catecholamine content, fiber counts of visceral efferent nerves, and conduction velocity studies on single units.

The implication of these findings for the whole organism is that many of the age-related observations can be partially explained on the basis of increased nerve thresholds. This would result in age-related performance deficits in those parameters requiring participation of the sympathetic and parasympathetic nerves. The longer time required by the aged to make responses might be caused by some hypothetical brain mechanism that sums stimuli until the threshold is exceeded.

The afferent limb of the VNS has received scant attention with respect to aging processes. Frolkis has again provided the most direct systematic data. He studied the change in pressure necessary to elicit a pressor reflex from the carotid sinus and found that these changes were 50 per cent smaller in the old animals than in the young ones. In additional experiments the sensitivity of vascular chemoreceptors to the action of hypoxia and cholinominetic substances increased with age. He also observed that the latency of interoceptive reflexes elicited by these stimuli was decreased, but the magnitude of the response was reduced.

While these data were obtained from anesthetized animals in the laboratory and therefore are not necessarily applicable to man, they have some interesting implications. First, interoceptors appear to be substantially more sensitive in the aged than in the young, a finding that confirms many clinical impressions about the preoccupation of the aged with bodily processes. Second, it appears that the observed decrease in cardiac deceleration in the aged, as obtained by Thompson and Nowlin, may have been an adaptation to this increased sensitivity. If the Lacey hypothesis of visceral inhibition is correct, not as much cardiac deceleration in the aged would be needed to produce the same amount of inhibition as occurs in the young.

Much more information about the effects of the visceral afferent system is needed. Several models are available. Populations of single unit neurons could be studied in old and young animals. Behavioral data could be obtained by using the carotid sinus denervation model devised by Ádám and cited above in old and young animals. Finally, data on chemical interoceptors could be obtained, using the example of Cabanac and Duclaux (1970). They found that the pleasant taste of sucrose decreased in some nonobese subjects after glucose loading, but no change in taste occurred in obese subjects. The results suggest impaired interoceptors in the obese, and similar experiments comparing old and young populations would undoubtedly prove fruitful with sucrose and other substances.

SUMMARY

While the foregoing data are far from complete, a picture of the brain-body relationship in the aged is emerging. It may be visualized as a closed loop with the brain at one end and visceral target organs, including blood vessels, at the other. They are connected by one-way streets consisting of visceral efferents, on the one hand, and visceral afferents on the other. Efferent traffic is limited to stimuli of sufficient magnitude to overcome the elevated threshold that occurs in the old; but once an impulse is initiated, it is carried rapidly. By contrast, the afferent limb is more responsive to stimuli in the old than in the young.

The brain processes information from both the internal and external environment and in some way selects which stimuli require either or both external and visceral responses. The latter serves as a stimulus for an afferent response. Some data suggest that excessive afferent visceral stimuli, at least those from stretch receptors in the cardiovascular system, may inhibit the mechanism by which the brain executes responses to both kinds of environmental stimuli.

This concept of the VNS-brain interaction is consistent with much of the observed behavioral data in the aged organism. Such diverse observations as independence from the external environment, learning decrements, prolonged recovery from illness, and preoccupation with bodily processes may be explained, at least in part, by the increased sensitivity of the visceral afferent nervous system to internal stimuli.

10 Systemic Disease and Behavioral Correlates

Frances L. Wilkie and Carl Eisdorfer

This paper will report on an investigation of the relationship between blood pressure and intelligence, as measured by the Wechsler Adult Intelligence Scale (WAIS [Wechsler, 1958]) in an aged population. The incidence of hypertension increases with age. In turn, hypertension may not only be associated with the development of cardiovascular disease, but it is also the primary precursor of cerebrovascular accidents, both of which are significantly more prevalent among the aged than among the young (Gover, 1948; Marks, 1961; Master et al., 1952; Pickering, 1961).

Numerous studies have suggested that essential hypertension may be linked with behavioral changes among middle-aged and elderly individuals. Enzer, Simonson, and Blankstein (1942) indicated that individuals with hypertension and/or coronary heart disease had worse than average flicker fusion thresholds. Apter and colleagues (1951), using the Halstead Impairment Index, found that hypertensives showed high indices of organic impairment, while Reitan (1954) reported possible organic impairment of intellectual functioning along

The authors acknowledge the support of PHS Research Grant HD–00668 from the National Institute of Child Health and Human Development.

with anxiety, depression, and hysterical tendencies on the Rorschach in subjects with elevated blood pressure. King (1956) noted that schizophrenic hypertensives were slower on reaction time, tapping speed, and finger dexterity measures than were a similar group of hypotensives. Birren and Spieth (1962) reported that a decline in speed among normotensive individuals was related to age but not to blood pressure; in other studies they have indicated that hypertension may be associated with significant psychomotor slowing (Birren et al., 1963; Spieth, 1962). In addition, Spieth (1964) has shown that a group of unmedicated hypertensive individuals performed almost as slowly on speed tests, including the WAIS Digit Symbol and Block Design subtests, as did a similar group with cerebrovascular disease, while a group of medically managed hypertensives responded as well as did healthy individuals. He concluded that the slowing in subjects with cardiovascular disease occurred with the more complex tasks and came in the "deciding what to do" rather than in the "doing" phase.

Blood pressure, which may affect cerebral blood flow, has been shown to relate to electroencephalographic (EEG) abnormalities. While hypotension is correlated with diffuse slow tracings, mild hypotension and borderline hypertension are more often linked with normal tracings (Harvald, 1958; Obrist, 1964; Obrist et al., 1961; Turton, 1958). Obrist (1964) contends that mild elevations of blood pressure may be necessary to maintain adequate cerebral circulation among the aged who have increased cerebral vascular resistance, and thus may have relevance for mental status.

Since hypertension may be present for years prior to the onset of more severe complications (i.e., cardiovascular disease or cerebrovascular accidents), it is surprising that in recent years little attention has been paid to the more subtle behavioral changes connected with elevations of blood pressure among the aged. The health status of elderly individuals is of relevance in investigation of intellectual decline among the aged, particularly since the two major developmental research strategies have shown contradictory findings. Cross-sectional studies have indicated age-related postmaturity decline (Wechsler, 1958), while longitudinal investigations have shown relatively stable intellectual performance over time or even some gains (Eisdorfer, 1968; Jarvik and Falek, 1963; Jarvik et al., 1957). Although any number of factors may account for this discrepancy, it is possible that poor health may be one of the major underlying causes, since the cross-sectional approach would be likely to include a larger proportion of the diseased and disabled among the aged than would be found in long-term follow-up investigations (Falek et al., 1960; Guilford, 1967; Jarvik and Blum, 1971; Jarvik et al., in press; Jarvik et al., 1962; Riegel et al., 1967).

In this report a cross-sectional strategy was employed to examine the relation between blood pressure and intelligence, with the results stemming from a ten-year longitudinal study of aging. Although all individuals who were tested in this program had initially agreed to participate in a long-term research project, there was a substantial loss of subjects (Ss) after each of the four examinations, due to illness, death, etc. In order to include a larger number of Ss with poor health (i.e., high blood pressure), this study used a cross-sectional technique to examine the results from the first and second examinations and included all individuals who had a given examination regardless of whether or not they returned for subsequent evaluations.

METHOD

Subjects

The volunteer Ss, aged 60-79, were recruited from the community to be participants in a longitudinal, multidisciplinary study at the Duke University Center for the Study of Aging and Human Development. Although these Ss do not represent a random sample, their sex, race, and socioeconomic characteristics approximate those in the Durham, North Carolina, area (Heyman and Jeffers, 1964).

The Ss were divided into two age groups, based upon their age at the initial evaluation. In the 60-69 age group there were 122 Ss who participated in the initial testing and 91 Ss who returned for the second examination (mean age 64.1 and 67.6 years, respectively). In the 70-79 age group there were 107 Ss at the first and 76 Ss at the second examination (mean age 72.2 and 75.2 years, respectively).

Examination Procedures

Although the Ss were evaluated four times during a ten-year period at intervals of two to three years, the focus in this report is on the first and second examinations, which were separated by a three-year interval.

Each evaluation consisted of two days of testing at the Medical Center, where all Ss underwent a complete physical and psychiatric examination, various laboratory tests, a social history interview, and numerous psychological tests, including the complete Wechsler Adult Intelligence Scale. As described elsewhere (Busse, 1965), Ss were not admitted to the hospital but were transported from and returned to their homes each day. It should be stressed that the project was not designed specifically to investigate the relation between blood pressure (BP) and intelligence; rather, the BP values were obtained during the routine physical examination and the WAIS was one of several psychological tests administered.

The BP values were obtained by standard auscultation technique, with the individual in a recumbent position. Systolic rather than diastolic BP was used since there was a high correlation ($p<.01$) between the two measures within the study, with a product moment correlation of approximately .80 for each age group. Similarly, findings from the Framingham (Dawber et al., 1959) longitudinal study of cardiac functioning indicate that systolic and diastolic pressure are normally highly correlated, suggesting that the two are equally reliable. The physician rounded the BP values to the nearest 10 mm-mercury (Hg). At each age level Ss were divided into three BP groups, which approximated Master, Garfield, and Walter's classification (1952) of systolic BP for the 60 and over age group and included: (1) a low group, with systolic pressures of 125 mm Hg and less (our range was 96-125): (2) a medium group, with pressures between 126-185 mm Hg; and (3) a high group, with systolic pressures of over 185 mm Hg (our range was 186-300). At both age levels, evidence of end organ change (that is, a cardiacthoracic ratio of more than 50 per cent on the basis of actual measurements taken from x-ray photographs and clinical signs of eye ground changes of grade II or III) occurred significantly less often ($p<.05$) in the low and medium BP groups than in the high BP group. Because of the nature of the study, antihypertensive drug usage could not be controlled. However, results obtained by Spieth (1964) suggest that such drugs would tend to attenuate rather than exaggerate any differences in performance between the individuals in our study.

Since the focus is upon low, medium, or heightened elevations of BP among individuals without clinical evidence of cerebrovascular disease, the data from seven additional persons originally examined in the longitudinal study were excluded here due to the presence of diagnosed cerebrovascular disease, to missing intelligence test data, or to missing BP values.

RESULTS

Table 1 shows the number of Ss in each of the BP categories at studies I and II. Each group included Ss from the upper and lower socioeconomic levels as well as individuals of both sexes and approximately the same ratio of whites and nonwhites.

For both age groups the relation between BP and intelligence was examined separately for studies I and II. A series of simple one-way analyses of variance

TABLE 10-1. Mean Age and Number of Subjects with High, Medium, or Low Systolic Blood Pressure at Studies I and II

Blood Pressure Groups	Study I						Study II					
	Aged 60-69 (mean age 64.1)			Aged 70-79 (mean age 72.2)			Aged 60-69 (mean age 67.6)			Aged 70-79 (mean age 75.2)		
	Total	Males	Females	Total	Males	Females	Total	Males	Females	Total	Males	Females
High	17	5	12	28	14	14	10	4	6	9	3	6
Medium	93	44	49	69	37	32	73	31	42	59	31	28
Low	12	7	5	10	5	5	7	5	2	8	5	3
Overall Total	122	56	66	107	56	51	90	40	50	76	39	37

compared the Full Scale, Verbal, and Performance Weighted scores of the three BP groups and included only those Ss who had all three Weighted scores. A second approach employed a product moment correlation to examine the relation between the actual BP values and the complete WAIS, and included all Ss at each subtest. While the correlations included all subjects, three Ss at each age level had to be excluded from the analyses of variance because they were missing so many subtests in the performance area that they did not have prorated Weighted scores.

Study I

Table 2 gives the mean Full Scale, Verbal, and Performance Weighted scores and the standard deviations for the low, medium, and high BP groups at the initial examination.

There were no significant intellectual differences between the age 60-69 BP groups on the initial examination. In contrast, among the 70- to 79-year-olds, significant differences were found between the BP groups in the Full Scale, Verbal, and Performance Weighted scores ($df = 2/104$, $F = 3.8$, 3.1, $p<.05$; and $F = 5.0$, $p<.01$, respectively). The 70- to 79-year-old low and medium BP groups had relatively similar intellectual scores. In contrast, when compared with the low and medium BP groups ($df = 104$), the elevated BP group averaged 16 and 10 points lower, respectively, in the verbal area

TABLE 10-2.   WAIS Weighted Score Means and Standard Deviations
According to Blood Pressure, Age, and Evaluation

WAIS Weighted Score	Blood Pressure Groups	Study I				Study II			
		Aged 60-69 N=122		Aged 70-79 N=107		Aged 60-69 N=90		Aged 70-79 N=76	
		Mean	S.D.	Mean	S.D.	Mean	S.D.	Mean	S.D.
	Low	85.3	40.2	92.6	31.5	104.2	38.2	100.8	43.2
Full Scale	Medium	86.9	30.1	81.1	36.1	90.7	29.1	81.8	31.4
	High	81.5	34.4	63.3	26.4	69.6	34.3	58.4	17.1
	Low	56.7	25.1	60.5	20.9	68.1	24.3	68.5	28.5
Verbal	Medium	56.9	19.3	54.5	23.2	58.7	19.0	54.5	20.5
	High	53.6	22.8	44.3	17.8	47.2	22.2	40.9	9.6
	Low	28.6	15.9	32.1	11.6	36.1	14.7	32.3	15.7
Performance	Medium	30.0	11.8	26.6	13.7	32.0	11.6	27.3	12.2
	High	27.9	12.2	19.0	10.6	22.4	13.4	17.5	8.4

TABLE 10-3.   Product-Moment Correlations Between Blood Pressure and Wechsler Adult Intelligence Scale Scores

	Study I		Study II	
	Aged 60-69 N=122	Aged 70-79 N=107	Aged 60-69 N=90	Aged 70-79 N=76
Verbal Wt. Score	−.08	−.28**	−.21*	−.22
Information	−.08	−.28**	−.21*	−.20
Comphrension	−.08	−.27**	−.17	−.25*
Arithmetic	−.12	−.30**	−.20	−.26*
Similarities	−.05	−.27**	−.18	−.12
Digit Span	−.01	−.22*	−.02	−.25*
Vocabulary	−.10	−.22*	−.20	−.23*
Performance Wt. Score	−.10	−.35**	−.25*	−.14
Digit Symbol	−.02	−.26**	−.25*	−.15
Pict. Compl.	−.12	−.36**	−.24*	−.12
Block Design	−.12	−.31**	−.25*	−.18
Pict. Arrang.	−.08	−.21*	−.17	−.16
Obj. Assembly	−.05	−.29**	−.19	−.02
Full Scale Wt. Score	−.10	−.33**	−.22*	−.18

* Significant at the .05 level.
** Significant at the .01 level.

($p<.05$, $t = 2.0$ and 2.1, respectively) and 13 and 8 points lower, respectively, in the performance area ($p<.01$, $t = 2.8$ and 2.6, respectively), with these differences reflected in the overall scores ($p<.05$, $t = 2.4$ and 2.4, respectively).

At each age level, a product-moment correlation that was based upon the entire testing sample was used to determine the relation between the actual BP values and the complete WAIS (see Table 3). For the 60 to 69 year-olds, BP was not related to the WAIS scores on the initial testing, although all the correlations were in the negative direction. For the 70 to 79 year-olds, the Full Scale, Verbal, and Performance Weighted scores, as well as all the subtests, were negatively correlated with BP at the .05 level or less.

Thus, on the initial examination, high BP was associated with low intelligence test scores at the older but not at the younger age.

Study II

From the group of 229 Ss examined at Study I, 91 and 76 Ss who were first tested at age 60–69 and 70–79, respectively, returned for a second evaluation.

Although no statistical differences were found in the verbal and overall scores between the three BP groups in the 60- to 69-year-old range, the elevated BP group tended to have the lowest scores in these areas (see Table 2). By contrast, in the performance area ($F = 3.5$, $df = 2/85$, $p<.05$), the elevated BP group in the 60-69 age range averaged 14 and 10 points lower than the low and medium BP groups, respectively ($df = 85$, $p<.05$, $t = 2.3$ and 2.2, respectively). Among the 70- to 79-year-olds, significant differences were found between the BP groups in the Verbal, Performance, and Full Scale Weighted scores ($df = 2/70$, $F = 3.6$, 3.1, and 3.6, respectively; $p<.05$). Thus, the 70- to 79-year-old elevated pressure group averaged 28 points lower in the verbal area ($t = 2.7$, $df = 70$, $p<.01$) and 15 points lower in performance score ($t = 2.4$, $p<.05$) than the low pressure group, with this difference reflected in the Full Scale score ($t = 2.7$, $p<.01$). On the other hand, the elevated pressure group differed significantly from the medium BP group only in the performance area ($t = 2.1$, $df = 70$, $p<.05$).

Shown in Table 3 are the product-moment correlations between BP and the complete WAIS at the second examination. While the analysis of variance approach was limited only to those Ss who had the Verbal, Performance, and Full Scale Weighted scores, the correlations included the entire testing sample at each subtest, independent of whether the Ss had all three WAIS Weighted scores. Thus, at each age level the correlations included three additional Ss who had some of the Performance subtests but did not have the Performance Weighted score. The correlations indicate that among the 60 to 69 year-olds, BP was negatively related to the Verbal, Performance, and Full Scale Weighted scores at the .05 level. Thus, the marked trend toward low Verbal and Full Scale Weighted scores among the elevated BP group in the analysis of variance results was significant in the correlation. At this age high BP was also significantly related to low scores on the Information, Digit Symbol, Picture Completion, and Block Design subtests. Among the 70 to 79 year-olds, BP was negatively correlated with the Comprehension, Arithmetic, Digit Span, and Vocabulary subtests at the .05 level. In contrast to the analyses of variance results, the product-moment correlations did not yield a significant relation between BP and the WAIS Weighted scores since only 15 per cent of the variance in the Performance and Full Scale scores was attributed to a linear relation and only 3 per cent of the variance was attributed to a curvilinear relation.

DISCUSSION AND SUMMARY

In support of previous findings, our results indicate that an elevated blood pressure may be associated with low intelligence test scores on the WAIS. The data stem from the first two evaluations of a longitudinal study. In order to include at the initial testing, a larger number of individuals with poor health (i.e., high blood pressure) who would be unable to return for subsequent examinations, all Ss seen at each examination were included. The results indicate that at the initial testing blood pressure was significantly related to intellectual functioning among our 70 to 79 year-olds but not among our 60 to 69 year-olds. At the second examination, blood pressure was negatively related to intelligence test performance among the 60- to 69-year-olds, but the relationship between blood pressure and intellectual functioning among the 70- to 79-year-olds was not as great as it had been at the initial examination. An elevated blood pressure was significantly ($p > .01$) related to S dropout rate after the initial examination among the 70 to 79 year-olds but not among our 60 to 69 year-olds. For the older age group, 60 per cent of the original group with high blood pressure did not return for the second examination compared to only 20 per cent of their age peers with lower blood pressure values. This differential rate of S attrition could account for the failure to find a relationship between blood pressure and mental status at the second evaluation among the 70 to 79 year-olds. In addition, since the relationship between blood pressure and intelligence was examined separately for the two studies, it should be noted that some of the returning Ss at both age levels (i.e., 60–69 and 70–79) had different blood pressure values on the second test than on the first examination, and consequently were not in the same blood pressure categories (i.e., low, medium, or high) for the two studies.

Since the dropout rate between studies I and II was related to blood pressure among the 70 to 79 year-olds but not among the 60 to 69 year-olds, it might be appropriate to ask whether some individuals develop adequate compensatory mechanisms to hypertension and therefore adjust to it with minimal difficulty for protracted periods, while others who do not develop adequate physiologic or anatomic compensations show central nervous system difficulties, with cognitive deficits and progressively severe physical pathology. In this regard, the presence of large numbers of aged with cardiovascular illness suggests that the rate of intellectual decline found generally among the elderly should be considered secondary to some pathologic processes and not merely an index of deterioration with advancing age.

ADDENDUM

Since this report was completed, an investigation (Wilkie and Eisdorfer, 1971) has been made of the association between blood pressure and intellectual changes over a ten-year period based upon a follow-up study of the

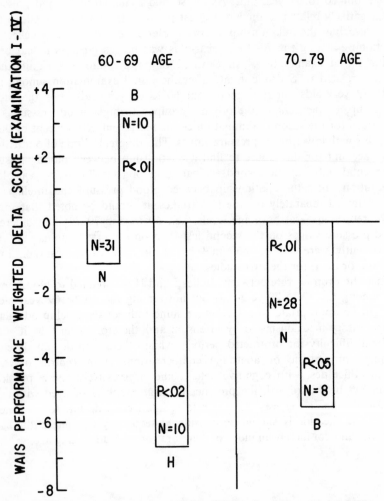

Fig. 10-1.   WAIS Performance Weighted Delta Score (Examination I-IV).

surviving members of the Duke sample who were first examined in the 60-79 age range. Included in this study were 51 and 36 members of the original groups of 60-69 and 70-79 years old, respectively. A shift from systolic to diastolic blood pressure was adopted in this study, since the diastolic pressure may be the more stable of the two measures, although the two are highly correlated. The WAIS delta scores (differences between studies I and IV) were examined as a function of the diastolic blood pressure at the first evaluation (Figure 10–1).

The results indicate that an elevated diastolic pressure was related to significant decline in performance and overall intellectual ability across the ten-year period among subjects initially examined at age 60-69. By contrast, their age peers with normal or mild elevations of blood pressure showed no intellectual loss. In fact, the group with mild elevations of blood pressure at this age showed a significant ($p<.01$) increase in the performance area of the WAIS. For the group initially examined at age 70-79 the results were less clear because there were no individuals with elevated blood pressure who completed the follow-up study and those with normal or mildly elevated pressure had some intellectual loss over the ten-year period. A comparison of the *initial* test scores of the survivors of the program with those of the non-survivors indicated that hypertension was related to low intelligence test scores only among those who *S*s did not subsequently complete the ten-year study.

11 Cerebral Correlates of Intellectual Function in Senescence

H. Shan Wang

In old age, the brain may undergo many structural and functional changes. Whether these changes are solely the effect of chronological age or also of some intracerebral or extracerebral pathological process is still in dispute. The effects of these changes on the behavior of old persons are also uncertain. As intellectual function often tends to decline progressively with advancing age and since many brain lesions are known to affect mental ability, a close relationship between level of intellectual performance and degree of integrity of the brain is hypothesized. This paper will present some evidence for such a hypothesis, but with no intention of being an exhaustive review of this topic.

HISTOPATHOLOGICAL STUDIES

The biopsy of brain tissue would seem to provide an excellent opportunity

The author acknowledges the support of Grant HD–00668 to the Duke University Center for the Study of Aging and Human Development.

for direct study of cerebral senile changes. However, in addition to the obvious practical difficulties, such an approach is not always as informative as expected. In a study of presenile dementia, Sim and his co-workers (1966) could find only nonspecific tissue changes in 17 of their 59 biopsy cases. With regard to intellectual function, they noted that patients with Alzheimer's disease had a tendency, during psychological testing, to show catastrophic reaction. The profile of the Wechsler Intelligence Scale for the Alzheimer's disease was somewhat different from that for other dementias: the former showed a greater impairment in all performance subtests than the latter.

In contrast to the above-mentioned biopsy studies, most morphological data about the senile brain have been provided by postmortem examination. The relationships between pathological findings and clinical manifestations of dementia are inconsistent. This inconsistency is to a great extent a result of the variation in criteria and methods employed. Rothschild (1937) could find no correlation between the degree of intellectual deterioration and the intensity of histopathological changes of the senile brain, e.g., cell loss, formation of senile plaques, and neurofibrillary degeneration. Riese (1946) concluded from his study that neither the degree of cortical atrophy nor the extent of cell destruction was proportionate to the duration of clinical history. On the other hand, Corsellis (1962) demonstrated that, with few exceptions, there was a good agreement between pathological finding and clinical diagnosis. Senile cerebral changes of moderate to severe degree, as indicated by a relatively marked cerebral atrophy, abundance of senile plaques, and neurofibrillary degeneration, were observed more often among patients having a clinical diagnosis of senile psychosis than among those who had been diagnosed as functional psychosis or as psychosis associated with cerebral vascular change. Grünthal (1930) reported that there was a parallelism between the severity of clinical manifestation of dementia and the number of senile plaques and neurofibrillary degeneration or the degree of cerebral atrophy. The most convincing evidence of a relationship between intellectual deterioration and cerebral senile changes by far was presented by Roth and his co-workers (1967). They employed a clinical scale and several simple psychological tests to evaluate quantitatively the degree of dementia in 60 senile patients, and subsequently studied postmortem the intensity of senile brain changes by counting the number of senile plaques in each microscopic field. They showed that a highly significant correlation was present between mean plaque counts and the severity of dementia, but only in less demented rather than in markedly demented subjects.

Pneumoencephalographic Studies

As an alternative to the histological approach, pneumoencephalographic studies can provide some morphological information on the senile brain *in vivo*. Definite evidence of cortical atrophy is present in almost all patients with senile or presenile dementia and is in good agreement with the clinical or psychological assessment of intellectual impairment (Gosling, 1955; Haug, 1962). This is further supported by the work of Nielsen and his co-workers (1966), who carried out air studies and psychological evaluations of intellectual impairment with a battery of tests on 300 neurological patients. They found that age and intellectual impairment were correlated closely with diffuse cortical atrophy, particularly that of the frontal lobe. Whether a similar relationship can also be demonstrated in healthy elderly with no apparent neurological disorders is unknown. The availability of less traumatic procedure, such as echoencephalography, and its possible use in determining ventricular size (Erba and Lombroso, 1968; Garg and Taylor, 1968) may help to clarify this problem in the future.

Electroencephalographic Studies

Clinically the evaluation of senile brain depends heavily on EEG studies (Busse and Wang, 1965). The literature on the relationship between EEG and intelligence is voluminous and has been extensively reviewed (Ellingson, 1956; Vogel and Broverman, 1964). Again, the data so far available are inconsistent. It appears that there is little or no relationship between these two when they are within normal limits. On the other hand, in the presence of organic disorder of the brain, a correlation between EEG abnormalities and intellectual impairment is likely to be present. Table 1 is a summary of several EEG studies on old persons, in which psychological measures, instead of clinical examinations, were employed in the evaluation of intellectual function. A correlation between EEG, particularly its dominant frequency, and intellectual function was present in almost all studies on residents of old-age homes and patients with various brain pathologies, psychiatric or medical disease. By contrast, such a correlation was exceptional among community volunteers who as a rule had better health and little brain pathology or

TABLE 11–1.   Summary of Studies on the Relationship Between EEG and
Psychological Test Results in Aged Persons

	Significant Relationship Between EEG and Psychological Test Results:	
Type of Subjects	*Absent*	*Present*
Community vounteers	Busse et al., 1956 (Wechsler)	Thaler, 1956 (Wechsler)
	Obrist et al., 1962 (Wechsler)	
	Birren et al., 1963 (Wechsler and others)	
Residents of old age home	Mundy-Castle, 1962 (Wechsler)	Hoagland, 1954 (memory scores)
		Ermentini & Marinato, 1960 (Raven)
		Obrist et al., 1962 (Wechsler)
		Justiss, 1962 (Porteus Maze)
Patients, medical and psychiatric		
brain disease excluded	Bauer et al., 1966 (Wechsler)	
brain disease included		Silverman et al., 1953 (Wechsler)
		Hoagland, 1954 (memory scores)
		Bauer et al., 1966 (Wechsler)
		Ingram, 1966 (learning)
		Bankler, 1967 (Wechsler)

intellectual deterioration, although their EEGs tended to have a slower frequency than that of healthy young adults; about one-third of these community volunteers also showed some focal disturbances (Busse and Wang, 1965). The exception was Thaler's finding (1956), in which subjects (*S*s) with normal EEGs obtained a significantly higher Wechsler score than those with mixed or diffuse records. Thompson and Wilson (1966) also reported a relationship between verbal learning and electrocortical reactivity. They found that good learners had significantly faster waves during eye opening and photic stimulation than poor learners.

Findings of the Duke Longitudinal Project
   In a longitudinal study of a group of community volunteers who were repeatedly given EEG and WAIS study as well as a thorough physical and

laboratory examination at the Duke University Center for the Study of Aging and Human Development, the author found 32 Ss who had had an education of 12 years or more (mean = 15.8 years) and were also free from any clinical evidence of cardiopulmonary and neurological disease at both studies I and II. The mean interval between the two studies was 3.5 years.

At Study I the dominant rhythm in occipital tracings was measurable in 27 of their EEGs. For these 27 Ss, who were predominantly Caucasian (N = 24) and male (N = 16) and had a mean age of 70.1 years, the mean frequency of their dominant rhythms was 9.5 cycles per second. There was no significant relationship between dominant frequency and WAIS scaled scores. Para-doxically the slower frequency tended to associate with a higher verbal score, and hence there was a negative correlation between frequency and verbal performance discrepancy ($r = -0.61$, $p < 0.01$). This was probably due in part to a difference in education. Ss with frequency of 8.9 cycles or less (N = 5) were found to have an average of two more years of education than subjects with faster dominant frequency.

At Study II the verbal and performance scaled scores of these 27 Ss declined an average of 1 and 1.4 points, respectively. The slower EEG frequency at Study I was significantly associated with a greater decline in performance ($r = .43$, $p < 0.05$), but not in verbal scores. Neither WAIS changes, verbal or performance, were related to their initial value or to changes of EEG frequency during this period of time.

Initially 14 EEGs (13 with measurable dominant rhythm) showed focal disturbances consisting of predominantly theta or delta waves over the left anterior temporal region. The group with foci, and the normal group that consisted of the other 18 Ss who had no foci in their initial EEGs, were quite alike in age, sex, race, and socioeconomic status. The foci group had a some-what slower EEG frequency and a slightly higher education, but neither was statistically significant. The groups also did not differ much in their initial verbal and performance scores (Table 2), nor hence in the sum and discrepancy of these two scores.

The WAIS changes from Study I to II are illustrated in Figure 1. A decline of one or more points of verbal score was observed in 10 Ss (or 71 per cent of the foci group), an incidence significantly higher than that for the normal group, in which only 33 per cent showed such a decline during the same period of time ($x^2 = 4.57$, $p < 0.05$). The mean change in verbal score for these two

TABLE 11-2.   Differences in WAIS Scale Scores between Elderly Subjects
with and without EEG Foci at Study I

| WAIS Scale Scores at Study I | EEG Focal Disturbances at Study I: | | | |
| | Absent | | Present | |
	Mean	S.D.	Mean	S.D.
Verbal	72.8	14.8	75.4	11.7
Performance	39.3	8.5	39.6	9.3
Verbal+Performance	112.1	22.1	115.1	19.3
Verbal−Performance	33.6	9.4	35.9	8.7

groups was also significantly different. There was a decrease of 3.7 points of
scaled score for the foci group, but a gain of 1.0 point for the normal group
($t = 2.29$, $p < 0.05$). The former tended to show a greater decline than the
latter in every verbal subtest except digit span. However, only the difference in
vocabulary was significant ($t = 2.76$, $p < 0.01$).

During this three-and-a-half-year interval, there was no statistically significant difference in performance change between the foci and the normal
group. Nevertheless, there were slightly more Ss in the foci group (as com-

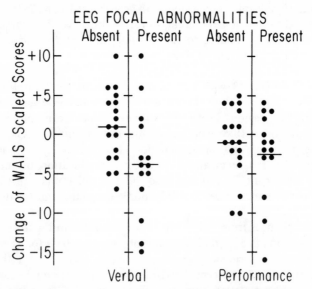

Fig. 11-1.   Changes in WAIS scores from Study I to Study II in subjects initially
with or without EEG focal abnormalities (Horizontal line indicates mean change).

pared with the normal group) showing a decline in performance scaled scores (64.3 per cent vs 55.6 per cent). The mean performance change of the former group was a decline of 2.5 points of scaled score, while that of the latter was a decline of 1.1 points.

Discussion

It is still uncertain which physiological or pathological processes underlie the EEG findings in the healthy elderly persons. The *slowing of dominant frequency* is a very common finding among aged persons with various neuropsychiatric disorders or organic brain syndromes. Some of our *S*s, in spite of excellent health, had a slow EEG frequency that was associated with a greater decline of the nonverbal intellectual abilities than was seen in subjects with faster EEG frequencies. It has been demonstrated in both animal and human studies that there is a good correlation between EEG frequency and cerebral oxygen consumption or cerebral blood flow (Obrist et al., 1963; Ingvar et al., 1965). The slowing of dominant frequency in our healthy *S*s may therefore suggest the presence of a subclinical brain disorder that is probably associated with a depressed cerebral metabolism. This hypothesis is further supported by the finding of an association between slow EEG frequency and low blood pressure in these healthy elderly persons (Wang et al., 1967).

The *focal disturbances* commonly encountered in the EEGs of old persons having relatively good health almost always involve predominantly the left anterior temporal region. They may begin their appearance in early middle age (Busse and Obrist, 1965). Although the incidence of these foci tends to increase with advancing age, it has been shown that, with few exceptions, these foci are quite stable after their appearance and are not related to any known neurological disorder. Our study did demonstrate a relationship between these EEG foci and the decline in verbal intellectual abilities. It may be speculated that underlying these EEG foci there is probably a disorder of the left temporal lobe, the integrity of which is known to be of great importance in verbal comprehension and retention (Milner, 1958).

CEREBRAL BLOOD FLOW STUDIES

The evaluation of cerebral metabolic rate usually involves a determination of the cerebral blood flow and of the cerebral oxygen uptake, on the basis of which the total oxygen consumption of the brain is calculated. In old persons with cerebral arteriosclerosis or organic brain syndromes, the cerebral oxygen consumption or the cerebral blood flow, or both, tend to decline. Such decline usually parallels the mental impairment (Butler et al., 1965; Hedlund et al., 1964; Klee, 1964; Lassen et al., 1957). By contrast, cerebral metabolism does not decline, or only declines slightly, in elderly with optimal health and there is no relationship between their cerebral metabolism and intellectual function (Birren et al., 1963; Dastur et al., 1963).

Most studies of cerebral blood flow use the nitrous oxide method of Kety and Schmidt (1945), which estimates the average flow for the entire brain. Determination of the blood flow—separately for gray matter and for white matter—of a small region of the brain has become possible only lately. Using a radioactive inert gas, 133-xenon, Obrist and his co-workers (1967) have developed an inhalation method for measuring the regional cerebral blood flow that gives a result quite comparable to that obtained by the carotid injection method, while all risk inherent in the latter method can be avoided. In this xenon inhalation method, the S inhales a mixture of 133-xenon and air for about one minute. The radioactivity of the head is then monitored continuously by two NaI scintillation detectors placed symmetrically over the bilateral parietal regions. The clearance curve so obtained is analyzed for its three components, and the blood flow, in ml/100 gm/min, for gray matter, white matter, and extracerebral tissue is calculated.

Findings of the Duke Longitudinal Project

The xenon inhalation method was used in a pilot study on 24 volunteers (12 males, 12 females) from the Duke longitudinal project during their fifth return for examination, about twelve years after the first one. The mean age of this group was 79.5 years (range = 71-87 years). The median of their cortical or gray matter blood flow was 55 ml. According to their blood flow, these Ss were dichotomized into two groups: one group with high blood flow ranging from 55.1 to 72 ml, with a mean of 61 ml; the other with low blood flow ranging from 32.5 to 54.5 ml, with a mean of 43.7 ml. These two groups were not significantly different in age, sex, race, socioeconomic status, and education.

The WAIS scaled scores were again used as an indicator of their intellectual function. The high blood flow group obtained a higher verbal and a higher performance score at the time of blood flow study and showed less decline in both scores during the twelve years prior to the blood flow study than the low blood flow group (Table 3). Statistically, only the difference in performance change prior to the cerebral blood flow study was nearly significant ($t = 1.97$, $p<0.1$). It was noted that most WAIS differences between these two groups were contributed by Ss with either low socioeconomic

TABLE 11-3. Differences in WAIS Scaled Score and Their Changes between Subjects with High Cerebral Blood Flow and Subjects with Low Cerebral Blood Flow

| | Cortical Blood Flow (ml/100gm/min) | | | |
| | High (N=12) | | Low (N=12) | |
WAIS Scaled Scores	Mean	S.D.	Mean	S.D.
At CBF Study				
Verbal	57.3	18.3	54.0	22.8
Performance	28.3	10.6	22.2	13.4
Total	85.6	26.6	76.2	23.3
Changes before CBF Study				
(12 years)				
Verbal	−1.1	3.3	−5.8	14.4
Performance	−0.6	3.7	−6.6	9.4
Total	−1.8	4.8	−12.3	23.3

status or low education (the latter was arbitrarily defined in our study as an education of 11 years or less).

In the 10 Ss who had both low socioeconomic status and low education (Figure 2), both verbal and performance scores tended to parallel the blood

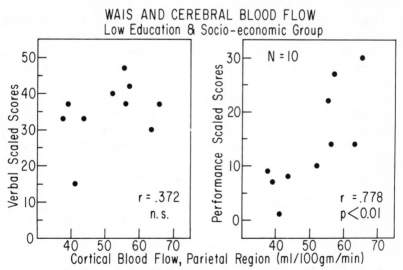

Fig. 11-2. Relationship between cerebral blood flow and WAIS scaled scores in subjects with both low education and low socioeconomic status.

flow. The relationship between performance and blood flow was highly significant ($p<.01$). In these Ss, lower blood flow also tended to be associated with a greater decline in performance during the twelve years prior to the blood flow study. The correlation coefficient between blood flow and performance change was $+.41$, which was not significant for a sample of 10, but was nonetheless much higher than that between blood flow and verbal change ($r = +.12$). A similar pattern, namely, that blood flow is more closely related to performance than to verbal ability, was also observed in the other 10 Ss who had both high socioeconomic status and high education. The correlation between blood flow and decline in performance prior to the blood flow study was significant at 0.05 level ($r = +.73$).

Discussion

The meaning of a positive relationship between blood flow and intellectual function is still not clear. The low cerebral blood flow may result from some cerebrovascular disease or from a decrease of cerebral metabolic activity secondary to a pathological process primarily involving the brain tissue. In either case, intellectual impairment may occur. However, the low cerebral blood flow associated with cerebrovascular disease, at least at its early state, is more likely to follow a fluctuating course or to be reversible than that associated with primary disorder of the brain. It has been shown (Fazekas and Alman, 1964) that patients with cerebrovascular disease show poorer hemodynamic responses to carbon dioxide, a known vasodilator, thus suggesting a reduction of compensatory reserve in the circulatory system of the brain. Recently, Ingvar and Risberg (1965) demonstrated that, in healthy young men during arithmetic activity, there was a significant increase in cortical blood flow over the central and postcentral regions with a decrease in the white matter blood flow over the temporal regions. Whether or not a similar redistribution of blood flow during mental activity also occurs in old persons, and whether its failure to do so has any bearing on their intellectual function, is unknown. A study of the vascular reactivity or the reserve of the brain under various stresses, such as hypoxia, will probably help to uncover and differentiate some senile changes at their earliest stage.

CONCLUSION

The evidence from the literature indicates that there is a positive correlation between intellectual impairment and brain impairment in elderly neuropsychiatric patients with various brain disorders. Our studies have demonstrated that the intellectual function of healthy old persons who live in the community also depends to a great extent on the status of their brain, as indicated by EEG and cerebral blood flow findings. Such a relationship can be demonstrated especially when the many sociocultural factors that are known to affect the intellectual function and its assessment are controlled and when more specific assessment of a particular psychological or physiological function of a region of the brain is employed. The value of longitudinal study is also confirmed by our finding that several brain variables, such as EEG foci and occipital dominant frequency, correlate more closely with the intellectual changes over a period of time than with the absolute level of intellectual abilities.

SUMMARY

The purpose of the present paper is to evaluate the relationship between intellectual function and brain status in elderly persons. The pertinent data in the literature and those from a research project at the Duke University Center for the Study of Aging and Human Development are reviewed.

The evidence from the literature strongly indicates that there is generally a positive correlation between the degree of intellectual deterioration and the degree of brain impairment (as revealed by histopathological, pneumoencephalographic, electroencephalographic, or cerebral blood flow study) in institutionalized elderly patients who have various neuropsychiatric or brain disorders. Such a relationship is, however, exceptional in elderly persons who are living in the community and are in relatively good health.

The Duke project was a longitudinal study on elderly community volunteers whose intellectual function was measured repeatedly by the Wechsler Adult Intelligence Scale and whose brain status was evaluated repeatedly by electroencephalography and the xenon-inhalation method for regional cerebral blood flow. The study revealed that, when the socioeconomic and educational backgrounds of these Ss were carefully controlled, declines of nonverbal abilities were correlated with the slowing of EEG occipital dominant frequency and the reduction of cerebral blood flow over the parietal region. There was also an association between declines of verbal abilities and EEG foci that appeared predominantly over the left anterior temporal region. The findings from the Duke project thus suggest that intellectual function of healthy elderly persons in the community is dependent to a great extent on the status of their brain. The clinical significance of the EEG changes and of the reduction of cerebral blood flow observed in these elderly individuals is discussed. The value of relatively specific measures for the evaluation of a particular psychological and physiological function of a region of the brain and that of a longitudinal reserch approach are emphasized.

12 Relation of Increased Attention to Central and Autonomic Nervous System States

Larry W. Thompson and John B. Nowlin

There is an abundance of literature reporting a decrease in reaction time (RT) with increasing age. A recent paper by Talland aptly points out that "the adverse effect of age on speed of response is one of the least disputed propositions" (Talland, 1965, p. 528). It has also been well established that both intra- and interindividual differences in RT increase with age (Obrist, 1953; Spieth, 1965; Talland, 1965). The suggestion has been raised repeatedly that closer scrutiny of such variations in a diversity of experimental designs, particularly those which monitor potentially relevant physiological variables, may provide useful information regarding this well known age-related decrement (Birren, 1965; Obrist, 1965; Spieth, 1965; Welford, 1965). The impetus for the series of studies to be reported here stems from this general framework. It is not the intention of the present paper to review the literature or

The authors acknowledge Grant HD–00668 for the funding of this research.

discuss in detail the pertinent theoretical developments. Rather, the purpose is to present the findings of ongoing research in our laboratory that have relevance to this general problem. By and large the data reflect preliminary findings of work in progress; as such, they are not considered to provide conclusive answers but may, however, lead to interesting questions for further research.

The basic experimental paradigm employed centers around two specific questions: 1) what characteristic changes can be observed in several select physiological measures as the older person attends to or prepares for the presentation of an imperative stimulus; and 2) are these changes, if any, related to RT? The three measures under investigation were heart rate, blood pressure, and cortical negative slow potential changes, all of which have been reported to show some correlation with RT in young adult subjects (Birren, 1965; Callaway, 1965; Hillyard and Galambos, 1967; Lacey, 1967; Waszack and Obrist, 1969).

Heart Rate Changes

Heart rate deceleration has frequently been reported in young adults in situations typically regarded as arousing (Darrow, 1929a, 1929b; Davis, 1957; Graham and Clifton, 1966; Ruckmick, 1936). In recent years a number of studies have demonstrated that heart rate changes in response to arousing stimuli may vary according to the nature of the experimental task, such that an internal direction of attention is associated with heart rate acceleration and external direction of attention is associated with a decrease in heart rate (J. I. Lacey, 1959; J. I. Lacey et al. 1963; Obrist, 1963). In a recent review and theoretical discussion of these findings, Lacey (1967) has suggested that deceleration may facilitate environmental intake and related behavioral functioning. Support for this hypothesis can be seen in the heart rate changes that occur during the preparatory interval (PI) in a traditional RT experiment. Beat-by-beat deceleration has been reported during fixed foreperiods ranging from 4 to 14 seconds (B. C. Lacey and J. I. Lacey, 1965; J. I. Lacey, 1966), with the slowing reaching its lowest point at or shortly before the imperative stimulus is presented, followed by acceleration to above-baseline levels over the next several heartbeats. Further, the rate of deceleration is negatively correlated with RT in the 4-sec. PI condition.

A question of interest in our laboratory was whether similar results would be seen in an elderly group. A more detailed description of the procedure and results of this experiment is reported elsewhere (Morris and Thompson,

1969). Briefly, 26 elderly male subjects (*S*s) age 66 to 89 (mean age 73.7 years), participated in this experiment. All were community residents in reasonably good health. A young adult group comprised of 24 males, age 18 to 32 (mean age 22.5 years), was also included. Auditory tones of 400 and 1000 cp were used for the warning signal and imperative stimulus. Each *S* was given a block of 40 RT trials at each of 3 PIs (4, 9, and 14 sec.). Heart rate and respiration were monitored throughout the experiment.

Table 1 shows the mean heart rate deceleration in beats per minute (BPM), from the warning signal to the imperative stimulus for the 4-, 9-, and 14-sec. PI conditions. Although the mean change for the elderly group was considerably less than for the young and less than 1 BPM, it was still statistically significant during all three PIs ($t = 4.38$, 4.49 and 3.04, respectively, for the 4-, 9-, and 14-sec. conditions). Deceleration was more gradual during the longer PIs, but the total amount of change was similar in all three conditions. These results are consistent with those reported by Lacey and Lacey, (1965) in a similar experiment, and with classical conditioning studies that reported decrease in heart rate during the CS-US interval (Geer, 1964; Wilson, 1964; Wood and Obrist, 1966). Although the heart rate change for the old group was extremely small, the findings offer support for a relationship between anticipatory situations and cardiac deceleration. The possible role of sinus arhythmia in the observed deceleration was ruled out by controlling for respiratory phase in the data analysis.

In the young group there was a suggestion that RT was faster at times when cardiac deceleration was greater ($r = -.31$, $-.34$, and $-.35$ for the 4-, 9-, and 14-sec. PI conditions, respectively). Such a trend was not as apparent in the elderly group, although all the correlations were in the same direction. The absence of a higher correlation in the elderly group cannot be accounted for completely at the present time. A considerably large between-subject variability in both RT and cardiovascular responsivity in the aged group may have contributed to the lack of relationship. It is interesting to

TABLE 12-1.   Mean Heart Rate Deceleration (BPM) from the Warning Signal to the Imperative Stimulus during the 4-, 9- and 14-sec. PI

	Preparatory Interval (sec.)		
	Four	*Nine*	*Fourteen*
OLD	0.92**	0.83**	0.73*
YOUNG	4.38**	3.66**	3.44**

* $p < .01$.
** $p < .001$.

note that visual inspection of the data revealed marked individual differences in cardiac deceleration patterns in the elderly group. Several Ss showed virtually no change in heart rate during the PI, whereas others demonstrated patterns of change quite similar to young Ss. It was also apparent that many older Ss tended to reach peak deceleration at some point before or after presentation of the imperative stimulus, and the frequency of such occurrences increased during the 9- and 14-sec. PI conditions.

The exceptionally large individual differences observed in the elderly are quite compelling, and the possible relevant factors accounting for these variations demand further study. One obvious factor suggested by the data was that the elderly Ss may have had increasing difficulty in estimating the time intervals as the foreperiod durations increased. Perhaps greater deceleration would have been evident in the means of the aged group along with decreased between-subject variance measures if more trials had been run at each PI.

Another question of immediate interest pertained to the association between heart rate changes and other behavioral measures, such as measures of cognitive function. As a first step, 16 of the elderly Ss were administered select subtests of the WAIS and the Halstead Categories Test. The Categories test is an extensive and detailed concept formation task in which the S is required to "abstract" principles based on size, shape, number, color, and brightness. Poor performance on this test is reported to be significantly correlated with cerebral dysfunction (Reitan, 1955). Table 2 shows the means and standard deviations of the test scores for this sample. The WAIS scores are within the expected range for a sample at this age level. The mean on the Categories test is within the brain-damaged range, which is also consistent with results in the literature (Reed and Reitan, 1963). Rank order correlations were run between these measures and measures of heart rate deceleration and resting heart rate variability. No relationship was found between WAIS scores and heart rate measures. There was, however, some evidence to suggest

TABLE 12-2.   Means and Standard Deviations of WAIS Vocabulary, Similarities, and Block Design Subtests* and of the Halstead Categories Test for Selected Elderly Group**

	Vocabulary	*Similarities*	*Block Design*	*Categories*
MEAN	13.06	10.56	6.69	88.94
S.D.	2.74	2.85	2.36	19.65

* Scaled scores
** N = 16; mean age, 73.4 years.

an association between heart rate measures and concept formation, such that the greater the heart rate responsiveness, the better the scores on the Categories test. Correlation coefficients were .50, .25, and .38 for the 14-, 9-, and 4-sec. PI conditions, respectively ($df = 14$). The correlation between heart rate variability and the categories test was .35. While these correlations are not marked ($p > .05$ for all), they are all in the same direction and of such a magnitude as to encourage further exploration of the possible relationship between behavioral measures of CNS function and cardiac "flexibility" in the elderly.

BLOOD PRESSURE CHANGES

The relationship between age and heart rate deceleration in this experiment poses questions concerning concomitant changes in other cardiovascular measures. In particular, the possible importance of blood pressure changes is suggested, since the interrelationship between blood pressure and heart rate has been well established. It has been suggested that the finding of deceleration during the PI might be accounted for by blood pressure increases. This increase, which ordinarily accompanies sympathetic arousal in stressful situations, may act homeostatically to decrease heart rate through baroreceptor reflex systems to the heart via the vagus nerve (Heymans and Neil, 1958). On the other hand, Lacey's hypothesis (1967) would argue that in such behavioral situations one might well expect to see a decrease in blood pressure concomitant with cardiac deceleration, since afferent feedback from peripheral arterial baroreceptor systems may have an inhibitory effect on cortical and psychomotor functioning (Heymans and Neil, 1958). A third explanation would view the cardiac deceleration as part of a general inhibition of irrelevant somatic activity via central processes during preparation to respond (Obrist et al., 1970); from this, one might infer that changes in pressure may be secondary to this process.

Blood pressure, respiration, and heart rate measures were obtained during an RT task. A detailed description of the procedure and results can be found elsewhere (Nowlin et al., 1970a, 1970b). Sixteen young men (age 21–26 years) and 10 healthy older men (age 67–82 years) were given 58 RT trials in each of 2 PI conditions (4 and 9 sec.). The warning stimulus was the onset of a white light, and the imperative signal was the offset of the same light. Intra-arterial blood pressure was recorded from the radial artery by means of a continuous flushing pressure transducer (Statham Model SP-37). In the 4-sec. PI, blood pressure and heart rate were measured for three heartbeat intervals before, and three heartbeat intervals after, presentation of the stimulus to respond. In the 9-sec. condition, heart rate and blood pressure measurements were completed on six heartbeat intervals before and after the imperative signal. The peak of the arterial pulse wave following each heartbeat was used as a measure of systolic pressure. Diastolic pressure was measured at the lowest point that immediately preceded the rise of the arterial pulse wave. A multivariate analysis of variance computer program (Starmer, 1967) was used in analyzing the data.

Mean diastolic blood pressure responses for the young and old groups during the 4-sec. condition are shown in Figure 1. The characteristic beat-by-beat cardiac deceleration for the young before and after acceleration fol-

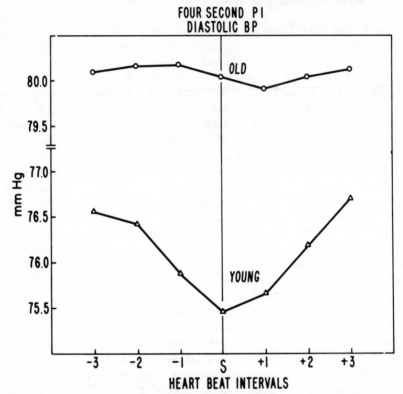

Fig. 12-1. Beat-by-beat measures of diastolic pressure for young and old Ss during RT task with a 4-sec. PI. Negative numbers indicate the serial position of heartbeats before the response signal (S); positive numbers refer to heartbeats following the response signal.

lowing the imperative signal was readily apparent ($p<.01$) but is not depicted in this figure. Changes in diastolic pressure parallel the heart rate change for both groups. As each beat decreased during the PI in the young group, there was a corresponding decrease in diastolic blood pressure; conversely, as heart rate accelerated following the response signal, diastolic blood pressure increased. Beat-by-beat comparisons revealed that all changes were significant at $p<.05$ level. It can be seen that the mean change in diastolic blood pressure is less for the elderly group and reaches its lowest point one beat after the response signal. Although the change for the old group was quite small, the overall test was significant ($p<.05$). Deceleration in heart rate during the PI was also significant ($p<.05$), though less than 1 BPM.

Figure 2 shows the change in systolic pressure for both age groups during the 4-sec. PI. For the young, there was no significant change before the response signal. Following the response signal there was a significant drop in

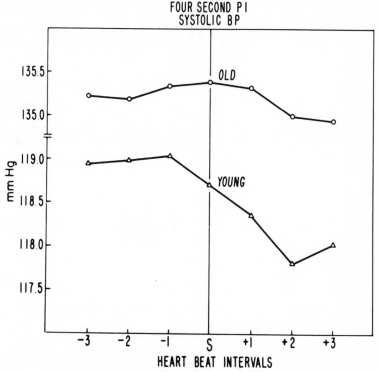

Fig. 12-2.   Beat-by-beat measures of systolic pressure for young and old *S*s during 4-sec. PI.

systolic pressure. It is interesting to note that although the pressure changes observed are quite small (in the range of 2–3 mm Hg), they tend to be consistent both across trials and across subjects. All measures following the imperative stimulus were significantly lower than prestimulus measures at the $p<.05$ level. There were no significant changes in systolic pressure for the old group, either during the PI or after the imperative stimulus.

The association between change in cardiovascular measures during the 4-sec. PI and RT was investigated by Pearson Product Moment Correlations. In the young group, heart rate decrease was significantly related to RT, such that the greater the deceleration the faster the RT ($r = -.539$; $df = 14$; $p<.05$). While the correlation between systolic pressure change and RT was not statistically significant ($r = .346$; $df = 11$; $p>.05$), it is sufficient to raise speculations about the role of pressure changes in response speed. The direction of the relationship suggests that slow RTs may be associated with positive or relatively small negative pressure changes, which is consistent with Lacey's

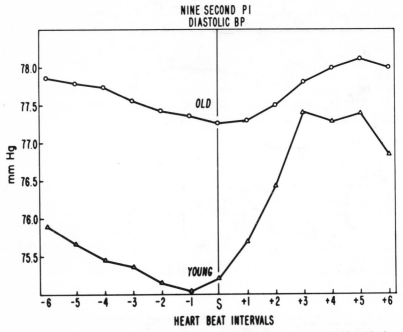

Fig. 12-3.   Beat-by-beat measures of diastolic pressure for young and old Ss during the 9- sec. PI. Mean pressure values were determined for the six heartbeats preceding the response signal (negative numbers) and for the six beats following the response signal (positive numbers).

hypothesis (Lacey, 1967). Diastolic changes showed little evidence of a relationship with RT ($r = -.106$; $df = 11$; $p > .05$). In the old group none of the correlations was significantly related to RT, nor were they sufficient to suggest a trend. The correlations were $-.02$, $-.20$, and $-.20$ for heart rate, systolic, and diastolic pressure changes, respectively.

Figure 3 shows the diastolic pressure response of the young and old Ss during the 9-sec. PI. In this condition six heartbeat intervals were examined both before and after the response signal. The young group showed significant cardiac deceleration ($p < .05$), which reached the lowest point one heartbeat interval before the response signal. Following the response signal there was marked acceleration of heart rate above baseline level ($p < .01$), which peaked at four beats following the stimulus and then declined over the last two heartbeat intervals measured. As in the 4-sec. PI, diastolic pressure changes were significant and paralleled heart rate in terms of magnitude and direction. The heart rate change for the old group was comparable to that of the young except that the magnitude was considerably less. The decrease during the PI was less than 1 BPM, but this was statistically significant ($p < .01$). The drop in diastolic pressure during the PI was less than 1 mm Hg, but this was consistently observed both between and within Ss, and was statistically significant ($p < .01$).

The systolic pressure changes for both age groups are shown in Figure 4. In the young group the pattern of change was similar to heart rate change, but tended to lag behind by about two heartbeat intervals. Though not so obvious because of the fewer number of heartbeat intervals examined, one can see a similar trend in the 4-sec. PI. It appears as if the systolic pressure response is similar but slower, and out of phase with heart rate and diastolic pressure changes by approximately two heartbeats. As with the young, systolic pressure changes were significant ($p < .01$) and similar to heart rate, but were approximately two beats out of phase in the old group.

The relationship between cardiovascular changes during the PI and RT was also determined for the 9-sec. condition. The between S correlation for heart rate decrease and RT was $-.446$ for the young group, which is not statistically significant. However, the magnitude of this correlation is consistent with other significant results, as reported in the literature, that were based on a larger number of Ss. Systolic and diastolic pressure changes also were not significantly correlated with RT ($r = .276$ and $-.211$, respectively). None of the changes in cardiovascular measures during the 9-sec. PI correlated significantly with RT in the old group. The correlation coefficients were $-.310$, $.153$, and $-.139$ for heart rate, systolic pressure, and diastolic pressure, respectively.

The results of these two studies lend support to the growing body of literature indicating that there are systematic cardiovascular responses as the level of attention increases in an RT task. The nature of the changes reported in the paper have considerable implications regarding the underlying mechanisms involved, but this is discussed in detail in another paper (Nowlin et al., 1970a). It is sufficient for our purposes to point out that cardiovascular changes for the elderly are dramatically reduced and show little or no relationship to RT in any of the conditions. Further, the absence of any increase in blood pressure during cardiac deceleration in the PI demonstrates rather convincingly that the characteristic heart rate change is not a homoestatic reflex reaction to increasing pressure. The significance of respiration as a single determinant has also been ruled out. It appears, then, that the observed patterning is in some way the result of CNS processes associated with an increased state of attention or arousal. Although not worked out in specific detail, a likely pathway for the mediation of this response via the autonomic nervous system has been well documented (Folkow et al., 1965).

If this assumption is considered tenable, the general picturefor the elderly suggests decreased autonomic responsivity during periods of arousal or focused attention. Such an interpretation is consistent with studies reporting decreased GSR responses (Botwinick and Kornetsky, 1960; Shmavonian et al., 1965) and decreased plethysmographic responses (Shmavonian et al., 1965)

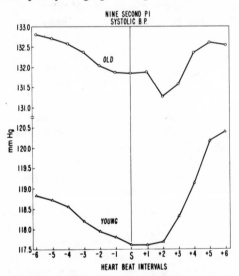

Fig. 12-4.   Beat-by-beat measures of systolic pressure for young and old Ss in the 9-sec. PI.

in the elderly during classical conditioning experiments using shock as the US. One problem here, however—at least with regard to heart rate and blood pressure responses—pertains to the possible uncoupling of cardiovascular and autonomic nervous system functioning with age as a result of structural changes in the cardiovascular system and/or other related end-organs. There is evidence of structural changes to support the hypothesis of decreased central autonomic reactivity in the elderly (Andrew, 1956; Nelson and Gelhorn, 1957, 1958), but it would seem that this is an area in need of further exploration.

CONTINGENT NEGATIVE VARIATION (CNV)

Recent work by Walter et al. (1964) has stimulated considerable interest in slow potential shifts recorded from the scalp. In a series of studies using DC amplifiers, they observed a slow rising negative potential at the vertex during the PI in a typical $S_1 - S_2$ RT paradigm, which was followed by a shift in the positive direction after presentation of S_2. They labeled this evoked potential change the "contingent negative variation" since it was contingent on the presentation of a warning signal as well as a signal to respond, and varied in the negative direction.

It has been suggested that the CNV may be related to such psychological constructs as expectancy (Walter, 1965), conation (Low et al., 1966), motivation (Irwin et al., 1966; Rebert et al., 1967), and attention (Tecce and Scheff, 1969). A number of studies have indicated a relationship between some index of size of the CNV and level of arousal and/or attention as reflected in efficiency of performance (Hillyard, 1969; Low et al., 1966; Rebert et al., 1967). More specifically, RT has been shown to be related to CNV, such that the greater the amplitude of the CNV, the faster the RT (Hillyard and Galambos, 1967; Lacey and Lacey, 1970; Waszak and Obrist, 1969). The question was asked whether age differences in CNV would be observed and whether the CNV would be related to RT in an elderly group.

Eleven young (mean age 20.5 years) and 13 old (mean age 68 years) Ss were run in a traditional RT task with a 3-sec. and 6-sec. PI. Ss were given 75 RT trials in each PI condition. The warning stimulus was a red light (0.5 sec. duration) and the imperative signal was a white light which remained on until S responded. EKG, EOG, and EEG were recorded on a Grass Model 7 Polygraph. The EEG tracing was obtained from a vertex to mastoid placement. Silver-silver chloride electrodes (provided by NASA) were connected to a Grass P17 high-impedance probe, which fed into a Grass low-level DC preamplifier. The EOG was recorded from silver disk electrodes placed above the inner canthus and below the outer canthus of the left eye. These were fed directly into a Grass low-level DC preamplifier with the time constant setting at 0.8 sec. A BRS digital logic assembly was used in programming the stimuli, recording beat-by-beat heart rate and monitoring RT. All physiological data were recorded on a TMC FM tape recorder for subsequent analysis.

Each S's polygraph record was edited to eliminate trials in which eye artifacts were apparent. RTs of the remaining trials were then ranked from fastest to slowest. Fifteen trials with the fastest RTs and 15 with the slowest were selected for further analysis. EEG and EOG data from these trials were averaged on a Nuclear-Chicago Data Retrieval Computer, and the results

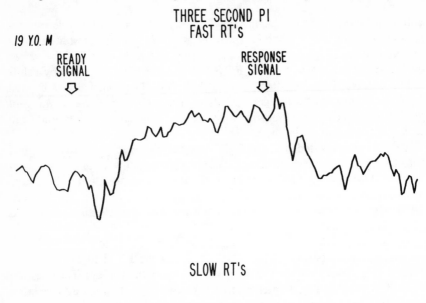

Fig. 12-5.   CNVs for a young S during RT task with a 3-sec. PI. Vertex to mastoid potentials were summated for the 15 fastest and 15 slowest RT trials.

were recorded on a Moseley x-y plotter. Five old and 3 young *S*s were eliminated from the study because of systematic eye artifact in the averaged tracing.

Figure 5 shows the CNV of a young *S* for the fast and slow RT trials during the 3-sec. PI. A slow rise in negativity is readily apparent following the warning signal in both the fast and slow trials. A shift in the positive direction is also in evidence following the response signal. It is interesting to note that the amplitude of the CNV continued to increase during the PI for the fast RT trials, but tended to level off and perhaps even decrease slightly for the group of slow RT trials; this is consistent with previous findings reported in the literature.

Figure 6 depicts the averaged tracing for fast and slow RT trials of an older *S*. Again a CNV is clearly in evidence for both slow and fast RT trials, which demonstrates rather vividly that older persons can have CNVs in the tradi-

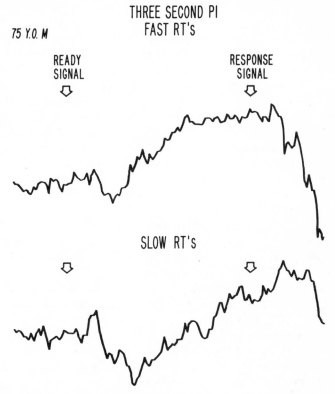

Fig. 12-6.   CNVs for an elderly *S* during fast and slow RT trials in a 3-sec. PI condition.

TABLE 12-3.   Mean Amplitude of the CNV (μv) for Fast and Slow Trials
in 3- and 6- Sec. PI Conditions

	Preparatory Interval			
	3-sec.		6-sec.	
	Fast RT	Slow RT	Fast RT	Slow RT
Old	13.9	12.1	11.7	9.4
Young	17.9	11.7	14.6	11.6

tional S_1-S_2 paradigm. In addition, there is some suggestion that the CNV for the group of fast RTs is greater than for the slow, although the difference is perhaps not as marked as for the young S. It should be pointed out that the difference between the CNVs for the fast and slow RT trials is more noticeable for this subject than for other elderly Ss who participated in this experiment.

Table 3 lists the mean amplitude of the CNV (μv) for the average of the fast and slow RT trials in both the 3- and 6-sec. PI conditions. The CNV measure reflects the average amplitude of the slow potential shift for 100 msec. immediately preceding S_2 relative to baseline values just before the presentation of S_1. It can be seen that the CNV tended to be smaller for the old than for the young in three of the four conditions, but this difference was not significant. An analysis of variance of the 3-sec. PI yielded an F ratio of 0.201 ($df = 1/15$; $p>.05$); for the 6-sec. PI the F ratio was 0.650 ($p>.05$). A comparison of the fast and slow RT trials revealed that the CNVs were smaller during the slow RTs than during the fast for both the 3- and 6-sec. PIs. This difference was statistically significant for the 3-sec. condition ($F = 17.84$; $df = 1/15$; $p<.01$), but not for the 6-sec. PI ($F = 1.22$; $p>.01$).

An analysis of the interaction effect of age and response speed was statistically significant for the 3-sec. PI ($F = 5.60$; $df = 1/15$; $p<.05$), but not for the 6- sec. PI ($F = .025$; $p>.05$). A close inspection of the means for each cell indicated that for the young group there was a significant difference between the CNV average for fast RT trials and the CNV average for slow RT trials ($t = 4.06$; $p<.01$). The difference for the old group was in the same direction, but was not statistically significant ($t = 1.16$; $p>.05$). A similar trend was suggested for the 6-sec. condition, but a test of the interaction effect was not significant ($F = .025$; $p>.05$).

The mean heart rate deceleration from the warning signal to the response signal is shown in Table 4 for the trials used in the CNV analysis. This includes the 15 fastest and slowest RT trials in both the 3- and 6-sec. PI conditions. In general, the results were consistent with findings reported earlier, and were more reliable than might be expected when one considers the few

TABLE 12-4.   Mean Heart Rate Deceleration (BPM) from Warning Signal to Response Signal for Fast and Slow Trials in 3- and 6–Sec. PI Conditions

	Preparatory Interval			
	3-sec.		6-sec.	
	Fast RT	*Slow RT*	*Fast RT*	*Slow RT*
Old	0.50	0.19	0.48	0.60
Young	2.48	1.30	3.50	3.00

number of trials averaged in each condition. The decrease in heart rate during the PI was evaluated by the Wilcoxen test for matched samples. The young Ss showed significant deceleration for the fast trials during both the 3- and 6-sec. PIs ($z = 2.01$ for both; $p<.05$). The elderly Ss also showed significant deceleration for the fast trials in the 3-sec. PI ($z = 2.00$; $p<.05$), but not in the 6-sec. PI ($z = 1.43$; $p>.05$). There were no significant decelerations for the slow RT trials. Age comparisons were made with the Mann-Whitney test for independent samples. The elderly group showed significantly less deceleration than the young for the 6-sec. fast ($z = 4.42$; $p<.001$), the 6-sec. slow ($z = 2.80$; $p<.01$), and the 3-sec. fast condition ($z = 2.10$; $p<.05$). The age difference for the slow RT trials in the 3-sec. PI approached statistical significance ($z = 1.92$; $p<.05$).

The results of this study clearly indicate that elderly people may develop slow negative potential shifts during increased attentive states, shifts that are comparable in many respects to those seen in the young. This finding has recently been supported in a pitch discrimination task (Thompson et al., in preparation). The failure to obtain marked age differences in the CNV is of particular interest, since it was observed in the face of an obvious age effect on cardiac responsivity. If one considers the notion that the CNV is related to level of attention and/or arousal, then these data suggest that the elderly were attentive and as aroused as the young Ss, at least with respect to this particular cortical index. Yet this attentive state was not reflected in performance measures; as expected, the elderly had longer RTs and, in addition, the CNV showed little or no relationship to response speed.

The age discrepancies between the two physiological indices under consideration, in combination with the absence of any association with response speed in the elderly, encourage some speculation regarding the interrelationship between the central and autonomic nervous system and its effect on efficiency of performance. Our data allude to comparable alertness or arousal between young and old at the cortical level, but the elderly are significantly less reactive (and perhaps less aroused) at the autonomic level. Such a conclusion is not inconsistent with the work of Shmavonian et al. (1965), in which they reported that old Ss had lower autonomic responses in conjunction with greater fast activity in the EEG than the young in a classical conditioning paradigm. The question could be raised whether performance might be impaired in the elderly as a result of antagonistic influences between the two systems.

In this regard it would be interesting to look at the relationship between measures of autonomic and central nervous system activity at varying levels of performance. The data in the present series of studies are not amenable to such an analysis. However, a crude comparison of our measures in this general context reinforces the possible fruitfulness of continued investigation along these lines. Table 5 lists the between-subject correlations of CNV and cardiac deceleration during fast and slow RT trials. It can be seen that the young Ss had the highest relationship between those two measures in the condition that yielded the fastest RTs. The rank order correlation was .929 for the fast RT trials in the 3-sec. PI ($p<.05$). The correlations during the other conditions, which yielded slower RTs, were positive but not significant. On the other hand, the correlations for the elderly group tended to be negative, and in the 6-sec. slow RT group, which comprised their slowest RTs, a respectable negative correlation ($-.670$) was obtained. While it would not be justifiable to consider such an analysis highly reliable, it nevertheless suggests that efficient performance is related to a high degree of concordance between the two systems, whereas a lack of congruence may be associated with poor performance as reflected in response speed measures.

Processes and structures that may be crucially implicated in this inter-relationship remain elusive at the present time. Questions could be raised whether this reflects a breakdown in the linkage between cortical and autonomic systems at the level of the central nervous system, or whether there is a failure in appropriate responsivity at the peripheral level. In any event it is

TABLE 12-5. Rank Order Correlation Coefficients Between CNV and heart Rate Deceleration for Fast and Slow RT Trials in 3- and 6–Sec. PI Conditions

	Preparatory Interval			
	3-sec.		*6-sec.*	
	Fast RT	*Slow RT*	*Fast RT*	*Slow RT*
Old	−.100	−.065	−.180	−.670
Young	.929*	.330	.360	.450

* $p<.05$.

difficult to ignore the possibility that diminished cardiovascular reactivity in the elderly may in some way be canceling the facilitatory effects of increased cortical activity during preparation to respond.

SUMMARY

The present series of experiments was designed to investigate the effects of age on selected physiological measures (heart rate, blood pressure, CNV) during increased attentive states in a reaction time (RT) task. A second focus of the studies was to determine whether changes in these measures were related to speed of response. Significant heart rate deceleration was observed during the preparatory interval (PI) in both young and old age groups, but this was significantly less in the elderly. A relationship between the rate of deceleration and RT was also observed in the young during the 4-sec. PI (but not in longer PIs), such that the greater the HR change, the faster the RT. A similar relationship was not apparent in the old group. A significant decrease in diastolic pressure was observed during the PIs in both groups, but again this was less in the old group. The diastolic changes tended to parallel heart rate changes, such that the slower the heart rate, the lower the pressure. A similar trend was apparent for systolic pressure, but this tended to lag behind and was approximately two beats out of phase. There was no relationship between pressure changes and RT in either group. A comparison of CNVs and heart rate in an RT task revealed no overall age effect in CNVs but a marked age effect in heart rate change. CNVs were correlated with response speed in the young, but not in the old. The possible contribution of central-autonomic interrelationships to performance decline with age was discussed.

13 Discussion: Mind and Body

Carl Eisdorfer

In recent years we have seen an emerging recognition of the importance of environmental and social influences upon behavior. While this interest has justifiably been broadening and intensifying, another long-standing area of knowledge related to human behavior may have been somewhat eclipsed. The countless attempts to cope with the problems of a mind-body dualism appear to have been resolved by many behavioral scientists in favor of a rejection of the body as an important locus of explanation for behavior. On the basis of a number of theoretical avenues ranging from behaviorism to social ecology it would appear that man is a collection of actual or potential behavioral output unbound by any somatic constraints. A psychology of aging which favors the stimulus-response view and ignores internal physiologic mechanisms is especially vulnerable, particularly since the physical changes associated with aging are of paramount importance.

Now that I have set up such a straw man, I would like to mutilate that pathetic figure. After all, no behavioral scientist would disagree that the nature and state of physiologic and somatic variables has something to do with the behavioral response repertoire of an individual—indeed, that they are inextricably intertwined. As is the situation with morality, however, we may accept the principles on a verbal level, but we find difficulty in practice.

The papers in this section are valuable exceptions to any tendency to ignore

125

the soma. A number stem from a set of observations that have been made over more than a decade, with many disciplines interacting in the evaluation of aging individuals in the community.

The studies fall into two categories. One focuses on basic autonomic as well as central nervous system activity and the behavioral sequela. Drs. Troyer, Thompson and Nowlin raise intriguing hypotheses concerning autonomic nervous system responsivity and autonomic and central nervous system interactions, as well as the patterns and mechanisms of autonomic and central nervous system response to such activities as mediators of behavior. In the other category, the studies of Wang, Wilkie, and Eisdorfer are concerned with the traditional display of cognitive and intellectual behavior and clinical-medical measurements. These investigators use the electroencephalogram or the indices of hypertension in attempting to study changes in intelligence and cognitive behavior over time.

The studies in this section, more empirical than theoretical, raise a number of important questions. How much, if at all, does intellectual capacity decline during the age span from 65 to 75 in the absence of any physical pathology? Furthermore, if adequate physical care were given these people, would there be a change in the level of intellectual functioning during the period of early and later senescence? What are the other relevant physical parameters to examine?

Overall, the papers focus on a range of internal physiologic processes from both a hypothetical and a pragmatic basis and attempt to solve the dilemma of "old versus sick." In a sense, they confront the "black box" approach to the aging process by demonstrating the legitimate role of the behavioral scientist in examining parameters of behavior change in relation to the state of the organism.

Among old people, in whom chronic and acute disease is more likely to be prevalent than at any other time during adult life and in whom physical change is an observable phenomenon, there is the very important possibility of intervention in behavior at a somatic level. There is also the very real probability that behavior may be an exquisitely sensitive indicator of physiologic state. Thus, the theoretical as well as pragmatic spin-off of such approaches warrants more intensive and meticulous study. Moreover, our concern with physical and biological ecology has had its social correlates, and individual behavior is being better understood in the context of the influence of societal and group dynamics as well as of other social system settings. An appreciation of the biological dynamics that relate to behavior could serve an important role in understanding and predicting behavioral change through an interaction of these variables in life settings.

Part III
Potential Contribution
of Life History Approaches

14 Design of a Comprehensive Life History Interview Schedule

Lissy F. Jarvik, Ruth Bennett, and Barbara Blumner

A long-term follow-up of senescent twins uncovered an intriguing relationship between survival and intellectual stability (Jarvik et al., 1957), a relationship which has also been reported by a number of investigators working with single-born subjects. While findings indicate an inverse association between cognitive decline and survival, the impact of other variables (e. g., biomedical, sociological, and psychological) upon life extension remains to be further explored. A major reason for this hiatus has been the unavailability of a comprehensive life history interview schedule. Our own data, for example, were recorded in anamnestic form at the time of the original contact, as well as during the two decades of subsequent interviews (Jarvik, 1969; Jarvik et al., 1962; Kallmann and Sander, 1948). The richness of such information is depreciated by the sisyphean labor required for its statistical utilization.

In order to test hypotheses concerning the many factors contributing to longevity and maintenance of intellectual abilities, a codifiable geriatric life history schedule became essential. The basic design problems involved tedious decisions regarding the inclusion or exclusion of specific items covering the entire life span of an aged individual and the selection of a propitious method of obtaining the desired information. Two general approaches guided the construction of the schedule: (1) subjective record keeping, as suggested by Daily (1958), who chronicled significant episodes and reactions to them, and (2) the more objective and dynamic one suggested by Bayley (1963), who stressed collecting data on patterns of growth and change by means of longitudinal studies.

Our life history schedule* was conceived as a standard comprehensive, structured, and codifiable interview to provide information on life experiences during childhood, adulthood, and senescence as elicited from the subject, his cotwin, physicians, and other informants. The following areas were covered: health, nutrition, critical maturational events, residential settings, activities and habits, sociability, education, work, and retirement, as well as demographic, familial, and genetic variables in addition to parental, marital, offspring, and sibling relationships.

The interview schedule was administered to the survivors of the original sample of senescent twins, collected between 1946 and 1949 by the late Franz Kallmann and associates (Jarvik, 1967; Jarvik et al., 1960; Kallmann and Sander, 1948), with a view toward defining the biological, sociological, and psychological correlates of longevity and successful aging. In addition, four criteria (independent of the life history) for judging successful aging were formulated: (1) physical health rated by physicians following thorough evaluation of medical records and physical examination; (2) psychiatric status assessed by psychiatrists using the customary psychiatric evaluation together with the Mental Status Schedule devised by Spitzer and colleagues (1967), including the Geriatric Supplement (Spitzer et al., 1969); (3) intellectual functioning as measured by psychological test scores (Blum, 1969; Jarvik, 1967); and (4) overall appearance, as judged by a trained observer, in relation to subject's chronological age (younger, norm, older).

A case history of the "C" twins (# A1014) will serve to illustrate what is meant by longevity and successful aging. Eighty-two-year-old N. and T., dizygotic twins, were first seen twenty years ago. At that time they were 62 years old; the disparity in their physical appearance may be seen in Figure 1. One of the twins, N., was about four inches taller than his brother, weighed 25 pounds more, had barely began to gray, and looked at least ten years

---

* Dr. L. Erlenmeyer Kimling, together with two of the present authors (LFJ and RB), was responsible for the design and construction of the interview schedule. Many others assisted in its development, including S. Goldman, F. Goldstein, E. Knell, V. Klodin, A. Kupperman, B. Novak, D. Pescor, and C. Weinstock.

Fig. 1.   The "C" twins (A1014) at ages 8 and 62.

Fig. 2.   The "C" twins (A1014) at age 82.

younger than his age. His brother had white hair and looked older than his age. Figure 2 illustrates the maintenance of their differential aging pattern in physical appearance, but with respect to other dimensions they both exemplified successful aging. They were both spry and active, and enjoyed good health. There was no evidence of psychiatric disorder. In general, their abilities as measured by the psychological test battery remained essentially unchanged over the years of the study. The observation above is indicative of the fact that marked differences in degree of aging, when they occur in twins, are seen in dizygotic (two-egg) rather than in monozygotic (one-egg) pairs and can be taken as a reflection of the genetic components of aging and longevity. Other genetic components are the high familial correlations for natural life span and the small intrapair differences in intellectual functioning exhibited by monozygotic twin partners, even when far advanced in age (Jarvik and Blum, 1971; Jarvik et al., in press; Kallmann and Jarvik, 1959). While the correlations are high concerning genetic components of aging, the interaction of hereditary and environmental factors in the production of age changes is still poorly understood. Therefore, in assembling the geriatric life history schedule, an effort has been made to isolate and document these interacting factors in order to clarify their role in successful aging and prolonged survival or, conversely, in morbidity and mortality.

DESCRIPTION OF INTERVIEW SCHEDULE

A. Biomedical Aspects

1. Nutrition. An attempt was made to incorporate detailed information on lifelong weight changes and dietary habits, including intake of carbohydrates, proteins, vitamins, sugar, salt, spices, and alcoholic beverages. Particular emphasis has been placed on saturated and unsaturated fats because of their association with arteriosclerosis and heart disease, as well as on caffein and sugar substitutes in the light of their reported chromosome-breaking actions and the possibility that such breaks predispose to cancer.

2. Health and Medication. Questions in this section concern health during childhood and adulthood including current health and medications, taken for a year or more, whether prescribed by a physician or self-prescribed. To aid in recall of information often neglected, specific questions are concerned with such medications as sleeping pills, tranquilizers, tonics, vitamins, laxatives and birth control pills, as well as with prescriptions taken for diverse symptoms like headaches, backaches, nasal congestion, and "stomach trouble." Also, smoking habits are examined intensively (because of their role in cardiovascular, pulmonary, and neoplastic diseases), as are changes in sleep patterns and in auditory and visual acuity. The latter commonly present problems in advanced age. With reference to specific illness, a list has been compiled including not only the diseases of old age, but also psychophysiological and a variety of other disorders (e.g., cancer, epilepsy, and tuberculosis). Information is being accumulated for the respondent and also for his relatives to detect genetic predisposition and to gain an impression of the health history of the entire family. Ages and causes of deaths are being registered for first-degree relatives and other significant family members, and, when possible, are further documented from death certificates and medical records. Any hospitalizations, operations, or accidents are being recorded in order to obtain primary medical data, whenever possible, from doctors' files and hospital records. This detailed medical and health history is essential in understanding the etiology of disease and in determining the role of various diseases in the dynamic processes of aging and long-term survival. In evaluating the interaction of heredity and environment in stress diseases, monozygotic twins offer a unique research opportunity; not only is genetic variability held constant, but age, sex, ethnic origin, and certain environmental factors in childhood have been controlled as well. We are aware of the deficiencies of any instrument that relies on retrospective data and the medical knowledge of lay respondents. With certain diseases—diabetes, for example—subjects may not even be aware that they have the disease. Documentation through hospital and physicians' records, together with current physical examinations and laboratory tests, compensates in part for these imperfections.

3. Activities. Included are questions concerned with the quantity and quality of activities as well as interests, habits, and community participation throughout the respondent's lifetime. The activities have been broken down into (a) physical activities, as illustrated by sports and gardening; (b) household activities, such as cooking and cleaning; (c) passive activities, such as television and card playing; (d) creative activities, such as writing and playing instruments; and (e) group activities, such as volunteer work and club membership. The questions have been arranged to distinguish the active, energetic person from the passive, sedentary one. Changes in types and amount of activity are also elicited to afford comparison between various phases of adulthood, including senescence, and to explore the relationship between activities and longevity.

B. Sociological Aspects

The sociological factors included in the interview schedule have been broken down into three key areas that are by no means mutually exclusive: social isolation factors, life stresses, and familial variables. Ancillary corroboration has been obtained for some of the sociological information.

1. Social Isolation Factors. It has been hypothesized that successful aging is precluded by a history of social isolation. Some empirical investigations of the aged population found that loss of contact among the aged negatively affects their adjustment. Others (Bennett, 1968; Granick and Nahemow, 1961) implicated reduced social interaction in the etiology of mental illness in old age. To test these ideas, the adulthood and current isolation indices of Bennett and Nahemow (1965) were incorporated into the schedule. The adulthood isolation index takes into account the number of interpersonal experiences during adulthood, assessing role relationships to the following: children, siblings, friends, relatives, parents, spouse, work, and voluntary organizations. In addition, the following role dimensions measured are: number, frequency of activation, and duration.

   2. Life Stresses.   It has also been hypothesized that experiencing numerous environmental changes over time (including change in socioeconomic status and location of residence), or experiencing numerous life stresses, is detrimental to successful aging (Simon, 1969). Life stress items, taken from Langner and Michael (1962), have therefore been included in the geriatric life history schedule.

   Some of the childhood stress items concern poor health in childhood, frequent disagreements with parents, parental psychophysiologic illnesses, parental "worrying," broken homes, and death of both parents. Among the adulthood stress items are illness of children and/or spouse, death of children and/or spouse, disagreement with spouse, divorce, financial difficulties, and job dissatisfaction. Old age items concern relocations due to institutionalization or multiple hospitalizations. In relation to "stress diseases" such as asthma, diabetes, rheumatoid arthritis, and hypertension (Srole et al., 1962), ascertainment of the hereditary, environmental, and emotional factors pertaining to organ specificity is important. Further, it is an aim of this schedule to delineate the role of the various stress diseases in morbidity, mortality, and longevity.

   3. Familial Variables.   Questions in this section pertain to the respondents' their parents', and their siblings' occupations, education, religion, ages, and causes of death (Cohen, 1964; Jalavisto, 1951). Marital history covers occupation, retirement, education, religion, and income of spouse, as well as details concerning sexual and marital adjustment, birth control methods used, pregnancies, and children (Burgess et al., 1963; Kinsey et al., 1948, 1953).

C. Psychological Aspects

   The following psychological hypotheses are being tested with the interview schedule and in conjunction with psychiatric evaluation and psychological tests:

1. Mental breakdown prior to senescence interferes with longevity and successful aging (Bleuler, 1950, Roth et al., 1969). Questions are included to cover lifetime hospitalizations and other indicators of prolonged physical or emotional illness, e.g., long absences from school and work.

2. The ability to adapt to change and stress is a requirement for successful aging (Simon, 1969). Thus, subjective "experiencing" and life satisfaction measures are included, as are descriptions of personal reactions to a wide variety of experiences and events over a lifetime—for example, reaction to loss of spouse, separation from cotwin, military service, and retirement.

3. Rates of development influence longevity. It has been suggested that persons who mature early show early decline and possibly a shortened life span. The interview elicits information regarding maturation patterns, including developmental milestones, ages at puberty, onset of dating behavior, and procurement of first job.

4. Activities, both physical and mental, maintained throughout life contribute to successful aging.

In the absence of adequate data, the contribution of physical and recreational activities to successful aging has been the subject of much speculation. A recent study (DeCarlo, 1971), utilizing information gathered on the senescent twins described above (see also Chapter 3), suggests that maintenance of cognitive as well as physical activities in middle and later life exerts a positive influence upon the aging pattern. The activity section of the interview schedule eliciting lifetime information on avocational pursuits (active and/or passive) made DeCarlo's study possible.

A brief case history will serve to illustrate the coexistence of stability of intellectual functioning and the maintenance of physical, vocational, and avocational activities despite changes in physical health at an advanced age.

Mrs. S. (# A1061) is a vital, self-confident, and poised 93-year-old woman who has maintained a quick wit, sharp reasoning abilities, and good motor coordination. Findings from repeated series of psychological tests administered over a 20-year time span show her to be alert, free from psychiatric disorder, and capable at levels considered to be more than adequate for a person 30 years younger. As may be seen in Figure 3, physically, Mrs. S. looks much younger then her chronological age. Despite the fact that she has great difficulty walking, due to senile osteoarthritis, she continues to be an active woman—seeing friends, supplementing the household income by crocheting, making rugs and mats, and collecting buttons which she arranges and sews into pictures and onto baskets. Her twin sister, although dizygotic, aged with comparable success and remained self-sufficient until her fatal heart attack at age 86.

Fig. 3.   Mrs. "S" (A1061) at age 93 and with co-twin at age 82.

The case of M. and L. (# A11414) illustrates that concordance for successful aging is not always de rigueur even among monozygotic twin partners who have identical genotypes; differences in life style may extend to differences in lifespan.

Mr. M., the conformist and observer of conventionalities, followed his father's bidding, and upon his marriage adjusted and conformed to his wife's ways and religion (Christian Science). He died at the age of 64, having been in poor health for two years prior to his death, without ever having consulted

Fig. 4.   The "M" and "L" twins (A6003) at ages 13 and 60, and survivor at age 80.

a physician. L. was more aggressive and outgoing. In fact, he took pride in being the rebellious one, and while economically less successful, he led a more adventurous life. Nevertheless, he maintained a very close relationship with his twin until the latter's marriage which strained the association but did not preclude the couple's caring for L'.s four children when his wife died. Now at age 87, L. is in good health and held in high esteem in an exacting intellectual field: he evaluates documents, plays, and books for renowned clients.

DISCUSSION

The New York State Psychiatric Institute Life History Interview Schedule consists primarily of close-ended questions that elicit past and present factual information about the respondent's life experiences as well as opinions and feelings about his life style. With a predominantly close-ended and precoded questionnaire, valuable anecdotal information is often lost, as are overall lifetime trends that do not readily fit into selected categories. To minimize this limitation, open-ended questions are contained in each section, and interviewers are instructed to write up anecdotal material and to comment on personal attitudes, morale, and outlook on life. A brief description of the subject's residence and life style, appearance (in terms of physical movement, dress, etc.), and attitude toward the interviewer and the interview is appended. The respondent's cooperativeness, lucidity, and seeming reliability are also ranked.

This comprehensive inclusive geriatric life history schedule is so constructed that the various sections (Marriage, Adjustment, and Birth; Family and Personal History; Nutrition; Activities; Health and Medications; Developmental Milestones; Religion, Education, Occupation; and Cotwin) may be used singly or in combination. For example, DeCarlo's (1971) interest was in the relationship between activities and successful aging and he used the Activities section alone. Each section of the interview schedule is very detailed so that it takes about five hours to administer the entire schedule. Since the ascertaining of such highly specific information is not always possible or even desirable, the Core Questionnaire was developed. It can be administered in approximately two hours and contains crucial factors from all sections of the life history schedule.

It is hoped that through the use of such a comprehensive interview schedule it will be possible to isolate and explore those medical, psychological, and sociological factors that are valid predictors of longevity and successful aging.

Moreover, detection of factors conducive to the maintenance of health during the later years of life should lead to the emergence of practical suggestions for optimizing the chances for successful aging.

15 Adaptability of Life History Interviews to the Study of Adult Development

Majda Thurnher

The life history interview schedule described in this paper was developed for use in a multidisciplinary study of adult development. The study focuses on changes in the interrelationship between two conceptual areas; the purposive domain (aspirations, objectives and commitments) and the behavioral style (the patterning of day-to-day activities, including both cognitive and affective aspects) at different life stages. Further, the study examines the salience of those two parameters for the process of adaptation. We also hope to explore the extent to which changes in purposive domain and behavioral style are attributable (1) to developmental or intrinsic changes within the

The author acknowledges the support of Grant HD–03051 from the National Institute of Child Health and Human Development.

personal system, and (2) to events common to successive stages of the lifespan.

Both purposive domain and behavioral style are viewed as manifestations of the interrelationship of the personal and social systems. These system in turn are seen as further major parameters of the study, to be approached primarily via the concepts of self-image and socialization. In addition, we plan to study the influence exerted on the purposive domain and behavioral style by such variables as physical and mental status and ethnic and socio-economic background.

The usefulness of this approach became clear during earlier studies conducted by the Adult Development Research Program. This work indicated significant differences in value orientations between healthy aged and those hospitalized for psychiatric illness, in that the healthy aged are characterized by the ability to reappraise and reorient their goals at times of transition or loss. Further, intensive life history material (gathered for other purposes) indicates that subjects with high morale expressed relative satisfaction with their past lives and achievements, whereas subjects with low morale gave evidence of failure in terms of reaching life objectives and of having held unrealistic and ambiguous goals. Our general conceptual and theoretical approach also borrows from the works of Murray (1951, 1962), who proposes that a few "ends which are desired for their own sake" can be ascribed to most individuals; Gordon Allport (1937, 1961), who stresses the central position of "intentions" or long-range goals for the integrity and health of adult personality; and Bühler (1959), who has formulated a system of needs for which she finds support in a study of life goals. More broadly, we touch upon "self-actualization" and related concepts found in the works of Kurt Goldstein (1940, 1963), David Riesman (1954), Carl Rogers (1951), and others.

The research design combines cross-sectional and longitudinal approaches. The sample includes 30 subjects (*S*s) of each sex at four transitional stages of the life span: high school seniors, newlyweds, "empty nest" (persons whose last child is in high school), and preretirement. Follow-up interviews within one- and five-year intervals are planned. Developmental changes in the configurations and congruence of the purposive domain and behavioral style will be examined through cross-stage comparisons, by follow-up study of age cohorts, and by the retrospective accounts of life-stage experiences from older *S*s.

We have attempted to devise a study in depth which permits dynamic interpretations without excluding rigorous comparisons in constructing the life history interview schedule. Our focus on goals and behavioral style represents a new conceptual framework, one that necessitates an open-ended approach, an approach that is also in keeping with our phenomenological emphasis. At the same time, our concern with obtaining quantifiable dimensional data that would lend themselves to statistical procedures led us to include structured questionnaires and measuring instruments as much as possible. Finally, the schedule has to be applicable, with only minimal modification, to a wide range of age groups. The initial interview schedule was drafted for the youngest life stage and was consecutively modified and expanded for later life stages, adaptation of the interview schedule for any later life stage thus being preceded by pretests on the antecedent stage. The final revision of the interview schedule consists of seven sections:

1. Sociodemographic Data Section. This is a structured questionnaire designed to elicit essential background information on such standard variables as education, religion, household arrangements, geographic mobility, occupation and history of employment, as well as basic data on families of origin and procreation (e. g., the age, education, occupation, and marital status of siblings, their location, and the frequency of contact.)

2. Health History and Psychiatric Symptoms Questionnaires. These are not conceived as comprehensive evaluations of physical and psychiatric status, but are designed to yield broad estimates of past and present physical health and psychiatric impairment. A systematic examination of developmental changes in physical status and psychological functioning is not within the scope of this study, and we are concerned with health primarily insofar as it affects activities and behavioral style and imposes constraints on the choice and pursuit of goals.

3. Daily and Yearly Cycle of Activities. This section consists of an open-ended interview intended to elicit a detailed account of *S*s daily, weekly, and yearly schedule of activities. Emphasis is given to the social context within which the activities occur, as well as to the satisfactions and significance that *S*s attach to these activities. Information is sought on the amount of time allocated to various activities and to the extent of scheduling and planning. This section is supplemented by a checklist of activities derived from responses of elderly *S*s in an earlier study and expanded to include activities engaged in by younger age groups. The comprehensive data thus gathered will constitute the basis for the formulation of a typology of behavioral styles.

4. Purposive System. This open-ended interview represents the central aspect of the study. It is designed to obtain comprehensive information on *S*s' current goals and aspirations: their nature and perceived determinants (e.g., the influence of events and significant persons), the actual steps taken toward the realization of goals, the perceived aids and impediments to their attainment, and the specific gratification expected from their attainment (e.g., the gratification seen to derive from the attainment of educational goals may vary: education may be sought to ensure a better standard of living, prestige, a meaningful occupation, and so forth). Areas of goal conflict and goal reorientation will also be explored and information will be obtained on reaction to externally enforced abandonment of goals and on the range of alternative goals perceived by Ss. In addition, subjects will be questioned on goals and their outcome at preceding life stages and on anticipated goal and life-style changes at later life stages. They will also be asked to contrast their goals with those of others—the goals of their parents when they were at the same stage in life, the goals of the older and younger generations. Lastly, the Ss will be asked to rank seven global areas in terms of current, past, and expected future salience. The rankings will also be made in terms of current activities and efforts directed toward their pursuit, as well as in terms of satisfaction with the progress made. The global areas to be sorted are the following: instrumental and material goals, interpersonal-expressive goals, philosophical-religious goals, social service goals, ease-contentment goals, hedonistic goals, and goals of personal growth.

5. *Social System.* A detailed exploration of relationships within the family of origin and the family of procreation, this section calls for description of the characteristics of family members, of specific modes of interaction, and of experienced and anticipated changes in the relationships. Friendship patterns are examined with respect to close friends' characteristics, the duration of friendships, and the frequency of contact and activities they involve. Information is elicited on organizational membership and activities and on subjects' awareness of, and involvement in, social problems and issues on the community, national, and international levels. The purpose of this interview section is to provide comprehensive data not only on interpersonal relationships, but also on Ss perceptions and evaluations of their immediate milieux and the wider social system. While problems of role models, the awareness of social norms, and the agents of socialization have been touched upon in the examination of the purposive system, the social system data gathered here lend themselves to further exploration of these areas.

6. *Evaluation of the Life Course.* The instrument used, the life evaluation chart*, consists of series of boxes arranged in rows of ten, each box representing a year of life, the total chart covering the years from birth to age 100.

---

* This chart is an adaptation of one developed by Professor Jean Macfarlane of the Institute of Human Development, University of California, Berkeley.

The Ss are asked to score each year of their past lives on nine-point scale, the end points of which represent "absolute tops" and "rock bottom." They are also asked to give estimates of the degree of satisfaction they expect to derive in the years ahead. The scoring completed, the interviewer reviews the chart with the Ss. Focusing first on the highest and lowest scores given and next on shifts in scores, the interviewer asks the Ss to describe fully the circumstances that prevailed at the time. The usefulness of the technique lies not only in the fact that it facilitates comparisons and permits statistical treatment, but also in that it lends itself to an assessment of the reliability of retrospective accounts of past life experiences, a matter that has perhaps not been given sufficient attention in studies of aging. Consistency and change in life chart scores between baseline and follow-up will be examined in relationship to changes in life circumstances prevailing at the two points in time, in order to determine the degree to which present satisfactions and dissatisfactions may affect evaluations of the past. In turn, consistency and change can be studied in relationship to personality dimensions: To what extent is consistency correlated with ego strength, or inconsistency with impairment in psychological functioning?

7. *The Personal System.* Our approach in the study of the personal system is directed toward the evaluation of both psychological resources and psychological deficits. The interview schedule includes several standard tests as well as a series of structured instruments developed by the Adult Development Research Program. WAIS Vocabulary and Block Design subtests (Wechsler, 1955) will be applied for the assessment of intellectual status; selected TAT cards (Murray, 1943) will be used for the measurement of such variables as anxiety, hostility, and social alienation, and will further serve for the analysis of ego-mastery styles (Gutmann, 1964); several measures of morale will be derived from the Bradburn Happiness Scale and the Bradburn Positive and Negative Indices of emotional states (Bradburn & Caplovitz, 1965). Additional instruments include a Symptoms Checklist (comprising 42 behaviors or "symptoms") constructed after consultation with psychiatrists and psychoanalysts affiliated with the research program, and an Adjective Checklist, designed for the study of self-concept, consisting of 70 personality traits to be rated in terms of real and ideal self and used also for interviewer rating of S. Lastly, the total narrative data will be used for global ratings of a series of adaptation resources, such as degree of intra- and extra-familial mutuality, resolution of losses, contextual and life-cycle perspectives, competence, insight, growth, and hope.

The administration of the total life history schedule requires 6–8 hours, and the narrative data collected are voluminous, if not formidable. However, the fact that we are embarking on a new area of research may be said to demand an approach that leaves room for induction.

SUMMARY

This paper discusses a comprehensive life history interview schedule developed in a sociopsychological study designed to explore the dynamics of life span changes in goals and behavior, social system variables, personality characteristics, and modes and levels of adaptation. The study seeks to determine the influence on developmental change in psychological functioning of such factors as sociocultural norms, value orientations, social system supports, and cumulative stress.

16 Discussion: Potential Contribution of and Current Obstacles to the Collection of Life History Data on Aging

Ruth Bennett

There seems to be no question about the need for longitudinal research which spans the individual's lifetime. Questions do arise, however, about the most effective and efficient way to pursue this type of research. Unfortunately, there is no concensus about how to conduct longitudinal studies and there are few, if any, examples of excellent research on a group from cradle to grave. This paper is devoted to discussing the potential contributions of a life history approach to research, some obstacles which impede its development and suggestions for overcoming these obstacles.

The need to locate one or more age cohorts at birth, or early in life, and to follow them over the course of a lifetime seems obvious from at least three points of view: the sociological, the psychological and the medical.

Sociologically, life history research is needed to determine the impact of social and cultural changes on a generation's life style and behavior. In a society in which social change is rapid, the sociological definition of a generation probably differs from that in a society in which change rarely occurs. Thus, in the U. S. a generation may span as few as ten years, while in primitive countries it may span a much longer time period. In the U. S. each successive generation, spanning only ten years, may differ markedly in health, values and behavior from the last, depending on a variety of social changes, especially in technology. For example, the current crop of 20–29 year-olds seems markedly different from 30–39 year-olds in several respects: They seem to use drugs freely, seem to start working at a later age, seem to be sexually and physically active, and seem very free-ranging. If longitudinal data were available on a random sample of both of these age groups, we might learn that child-rearing practices experienced in early life were related to current behavioral differences in the two groups. If we were to continue to follow the two groups, we might find that one group ages more successfully and/or lives to an older age than the other. To date, we have no adequate scientific way to determine how much of an impact social change has on the behavior, the health or longevity of successive generations of age cohorts.

From the psychological point of view, life history research is needed to describe the impact of a trait or a behavior exhibited early in life on other traits or behaviors which develop over the individual's lifetime. Many more discrete behaviors and individual characteristics are known to psychologists today than were studied years ago. For example, data are just beginning to accumulate on responses of neonates; were these to be supplemented with life-long follow-ups, we might learn if neonate behavior is related to adult behavior and to successful aging. Also, information is lacking on which behaviors span the lifetime and which do not, which behaviors remain constant and which change.

From the medical point of view, life history research is needed to determine if physical and mental disease, particularly if severe and chronic, result from, or result in, "pathological" styles of life.

For the reasons listed above, it would be advantageous to survey and follow on a national basis random samples of age cohorts at frequent intervals, preferably once a year. Such direct observation of processes and behaviors would also be more reliable than information based on recall. Needless to say, this is more easily said than done. We might ask why it is not feasible to study successive age cohorts over a lifetime. Surely, it is not because we lack the technology for conducting such research. High powered computers make it easy to record, store, collate and analyze life history data on random samples, if not the entire neonate population of the United States.

The obstacles which seem to stand in the way of life history research on a routine basis are:

1-Theoretical uncertainty about which processes, variables and end states should be studied.

2-Lack of methodological sophistication which limits us to the use of crude measures.

3-Lack of personnel to routinely collect and analyze masses of longitudinal data.

4-Lack of adequate financial support.

Once the obstacles are pin-pointed, solutions seem available, if not immediately practicable. Let us turn to the first obstacle, that of theoretical uncertainty.

In her paper, "Adaptability of Life History Interviews to the Study of Adult Development" Thurnher (Chapter 15) describes a life history interview schedule which "focuses on changes in the interrelationship between two conceptual areas, the purposive domain (aspirations, objectives and commitments) and the behavioral style (the patterning of day-to-day activities, including both cognitive and affective aspects) at different life stages" (p.137). The end state to be predicted was the process of adaptation. The independent variables or predictors were "the purposive domain" and "behavioral styles at different life stages." The intricacy of these three variables led to the development of a long (administration time 6–8 hours) and complex interview schedule containing the following seven sections: (1) Sociodemographic data section; (2) Health history and psychiatric symptom questionnaire; (3) Daily and yearly cycle of activities; (4) Purposive system data (information on goals); (5) Social system data (information on interpersonal relationships); (6) Evaluations of the life course, and (7) Personal system data (psychological tests and measures).

Jarvik et al. (Chapter 14) were basically atheoretical in their approach to the construction of a life history schedule. They designed one which was to be comprehensive and not limited to any particular type of predictor variables; the end states to be predicted were successful aging and longevity. The sample consisted of pairs of monozygotic and dizygotic twins who appeared to differ in the manner in which they aged and the age at which they died. Their interview schedule was "conceived as a standard, comprehensive, structured and codifiable interview" which contained sections on the following: (1) Nutrition; (2) Health and medication; (3) Activities; (4) Social relationships, including isolation and stress, (5) Personal history and (6) Psychological data.

In both studies mentioned above, the end states were sufficiently complex to require the collection of data on a wide range of variables spanning the individual's lifetime. Even though there was no concensus on which variables to observe, Thurnher and Jarvik et al. selected similar predictor variables despite differences in end states.

Despite the absence of a general theory of the life cycle, we should nonetheless be able to develop some guidelines for collecting life history data. Determination of which variables are crucial and which periods of time are critical should depend on which end states we wish to predict or influence. In other words, a core life history interview schedule can be designed, as Jarvik et al. suggest, particularly when concerned with predicting complex end states, such as adjustment or mental health in old age, to mention but two.

Some processes and variables probably should be studied only because good (valid and reliable) tests are available to measure them. Since there seems little agreement on which are the critical time periods for obtaining initial and follow-up measures, why not keep testing throughout the lifetime of an individual? There are some tests for which this is possible. There are others which measure a specific behavior, but which differ in complexity so as to mirror developmental changes, e.g., tests of cognitive performance. The only way in which nature-nurture types of theoretical controversies will be resolved will be by routine collection of both longitudinal and cross-sectional life history information. Thus far, it seems difficult to argue the merits of one theoretical framework, e.g., the environmentalist approach, over another, e.g., the organic approach, when two diametrically opposite research designs are used to test them.

In a review of the literature on cognitive performance in the aged, Weinstock and Bennett (1968) found that in cross-sectional studies, old people usually performed poorly on some cognitive tests when compared to young people, while in longitudinal studies they rarely showed significant decrements. A group of papers in this book, namely Rhudick and Gordon (Chapter 2), Eisdorfer and Wilkie (Chapter 4), and Blum et al. (Chapter 3) appear to bear this out. They report that, over time, when decrements in scores on tests of cognitive performance in the aged occurred, they could best be explained as the result of processes other than aging *per se*. Two interpretations of these apparently contradictory findings are: (1) Cross-sectional studies do not indicate the true nature of old people's cognitive ability. Possibly, this is due to the testing situation which puts old people at a distinct disadvantage; (2) Longitudinal studies do not indicate the true nature of old people's abilities. Possibly, they underestimate the cognitive decrements because the behaviors measured are trivial, or the periods selected for repeated measurement do not span enough time and may miss points of rapid negative change.

It should be reiterated that this type of apparent paradox can be resolved only by routinely collecting test data over the lifetime of successive groups of age cohorts.

The second obstacle to routinizing the collection of life history data is the unavailability of any but crude measures, applicable to the entire lifespan, and seen as critical for predicting important and complex end states such as successful aging and mental health in senescence.

Most of the available life history schedules are crude. For the most part they are unstructured, rely on recall of an aged person and self-reports. Little is known about the reliability and validity of the items used. Rarely are the data collected quantifiable in any meaningful sense. It would seem, therefore, that maximum cooperation is in order among behavioral scientists concerned with developing good, comprehensive and methodologically sophisticated life history schedules.

Thus, Jarvik et al. (Chapter 14) felt that there was a need to use, and therefore designed, a core life history questionnaire (administration time; two hours) useful in all studies, irrespective of the age cohort sampled, to which additional items or sections can be appended depending on the theoretical orientation of the investigators. While some of the factors studied overlapped in the papers listed above, the content and phrasing of items and observation methods varied widely: Thurnher (Chapter 15) relied heavily on self-reports, while Jarvik et al. used tests, measures and pre-coded items whenever possible. There are other life history schedules in preparation; one of these, Morin et al. (1968), relies heavily on open-ended rather than pre-coded items and concentrates on social relationships.

It seems reasonable to expect other scientists concerned with life history interviews to devote some of their efforts to developing a standard core life history to which sections could be added as new knowledge is accumulated. A standard and widely used life history schedule would mean that results would be comparable and interpretation would be facilitated. It is commonly accepted in most sciences that slight differences in method result in data which are not comparable. Before longitudinal studies are begun, perhaps we need to find a way of bringing life history researchers together to try to agree on the use of some standard measures and data gathering techniques.

The problem of locating, training and funding personnel to routinely collect and analyze longitudinal data on national samples of age cohorts seems to be the most difficult one to solve. Apparently, this is done with great efficiency in Denmark, where scientists are able to conduct longitudinal research on medically-related problems for which data are routinely collected. An example of longitudinal research based on Danish data is the work of Mednick and

Schulsinger (1968), which examines long-term impact of schizophrenic parents on their children. Longitudinal studies have also been conducted in Sweden (Hagnell, 1966) on the relationship of personality traits to serious physical illness in adults. Probably, in the absence of concensus on which stages or ages are crucial, annual testing should be conducted routinely on age cohort samples.

Few question the importance of longitudinal research to determine factors which predict successful aging and longevity. We should now begin to address ourselves to overcoming the obstacles standing in the way of formulating guidelines, categories and/or schedules for collecting life history data, perfecting measures of behaviors relevant throughout the life-cycle, and developing an organization responsible for ongoing life history data collection and analysis which will make these data readily available to scientists.

Part IV
Summary

17 A Summary: Prospects and Problems of Research on the Longitudinal Development of Man's Intellectual Capacities throughout Life

James E. Birren

The chapters of this book show the notable advances in research in developmental psychology that have been made in recent years. They also indicate that one of the most important questions the behavioral scientists can answer is, "How do man's intellectual abilities mature and age?" By acquiring knowledge of the relationships and principles of man's intellectual development we may expect to be able to minimize intellectual deficits on the one hand and, on the other hand, to maximize man's potential for creative adaptation to his environment during his entire life span.

For some investigators there has been a shift away from a focus on child psychology to an examination of the developmental processes throughout the life span. There has always been a greater emphasis in psychology on the early end of the life span than on old age. This is often justified with the view that the most important things happen early in life. As Sparrow said, "The beginnings of things are therefore to be looked into, that amendment may be made of that which is amiss, for one error there will hazard a loss of labour in all that is built upon it." (John Sparrow's Preface to Boehme's *Mysterium Magnum*, London, 1656.)* Such an inordinate emphasis on the beginnings of things, important though these are, tends to preclude the possibility that anything of great significance in our life span might derive from the influences of occupation, interpersonal relations, problems of health and illness, and the consequences of fortuitous events in the physical and social environment. Man is above all a highly adaptive animal and it is largely that property of his which we call "intelligence" that makes possible the wide range of his adaptations. It seems reasonable to assume that the very process of learning to adapt to his environment has facilitated the development of his intellect.

If we knew a great deal more than we do about our intelligence we might devise a machine that would artificially simulate or display it. However, one quality that the machine would undoubtedly lack would be man's adaptive capability. To simulate man's intelligence we would not only have to build a machine or system that would show intelligence but we would also have to provide it with the opportunity of growing and aging. If it is difficult to contemplate an artificial intelligence system that would simulate man's, how much more difficult it would be to expand such a system to include the goals and strategies of behavior that individuals acquire during their life spans. The full realization of man's intellectual potentialities requires not only a relatively error-free initial equipment, but the experience gained in developing appropriate strategies and tactics in interpersonal and interenvironmental transactions.

Despite the fact that a great many psychologists have become bored with the conceptual and operational difficulties of studying intelligence, the subject is far from dead, and the chapters in this book help us to learn more about it. Some psychologists would like to delete the term "intelligence" from the language and certainly from the text books that they write. It is certain, however, that there are great individual differences in how people solve the problems presented by the environment; we need a term for these differences and "intelligence" still seems useful. These individual differences appear to be related to genetics, the cultural environment, health, and that ubiquitous class of variables we label personality. This volume contains the reports of many competent investigators who have elaborated on the determinants of

---

*As quoted by Muses, C.A. The logic of biosimulation. In C.A. Muses (Ed.) *Aspects of the theory of artificial intelligence*, New York: Plenum Press, 1966, p. 115.

the large range in individual differences in intellectual capacity over the life span.

Fortunately, there are now a number of investigations that provide data on changes in intellectual ability over the life span. The longitudinal studies of individual differences reported in this volume provide us with valuable information about stability and change in intellectual function. One factor not commonly discussed in intellectual development in the early years of life is the relationship of intellectual functioning to the physiology of the organism. It has become apparent that if one is to study seriously the nature of intellectual change in the adult years, he must consider health a dynamic factor of greater importance than it is in childhood. This volume also contains a review of methods that can be used to describe the life history of individuals so that the content of the life span may be related to such features as intelligence and personality.

One of the problems for both a somatic approach and a life history approach to the study of the intellect is that one must select from so many possible relationships. The biology of man is indeed a complex matter, yet changes in many aspects of the organism, such as hair color and length, fingernail growth, or skeletal growth, may have little to do with thinking and behavior. Similarly, in the life histories of individuals there is so much information of potential significance that it is possible to get buried in trivia. While there is little doubt that there are still contributions to be made through a naturalistic approach to the study of development and aging of intellectual function, it is also apparent that investigators must know what to look for so as not to become distracted by inconsequential details. How does the investigator of these complex matters learn to concentrate on what is important? Investigators are products of their culture and induced in them is a sense of what is important in research. Our values also lead us to neglect some important problems. The problem of the criteria of adult intelligence has been notably neglected. Most intelligence tests and measures of intellectual ability in adults have been adapted from measures used with children or young adults. What abilities are most important in the adult years? Implicit in the use of intelligence tests based on those of children is the notion that intelligence is related to school achievement. This is not a satisfactory situation and a number of criteria might be posed against which to test the validity of our concepts and measurements of adult intelligence. Measures of intellectual function might be related to: 1) longevity, 2) occupation, 3) susceptibility to particular diseases, e.g., cardiovascular disease, 4) anatomic localization of behavior deficits associated with brain damage in later life, and 5) correlation with personality.

One source of individual differences in measures of intellectual ability is sex. Sex differences have not yet been adequately explored in relation to development and aging of the intellect. From the early literature it can be inferred that tests for intelligence have been constructed to minimize sex differences. What would be the consequences if we devised a test battery that would maximize sex differences? Also, what about the possibility of a relationship between intelligence and sex in later life resulting from the fact that women have much more favorable mortality rates than men? One would suspect that, if intelligence helps us adapt to our environment, then those qualities in women that lead to greater longevity should also be related to measurable intelligence. Is it reasonable that sex differences in survival should not be related to intellectual functions? On the other hand, if actual data were to be found that would show that intelligence in later life is no different in men and women, this would suggest that adult intelligence is rather more free of the influence of the somatic state of the organism than one might at this point surmise. There are further possibilities for research in cross-national studies. For example, by collecting data in countries of the world that differ in their mortality rates for men and women, one might obtain valuable information with regard to sex differences in intelligence.

Another area for research concerns the relationships of perception to intellectual function. In recent years, studies of perception have more and more tended to invoke physiological mechanisms in their explanations. Attention might be given to the measurement of intellectual processes by taking into account the results of investigations of perception rather than by limiting effort to the school-like test items inherited from child psychology. More particularly, investigations using the methods associated with signal detection theory might be used in the study of the performance of complex problem-solving tasks. This might help us to determine the extent to which limitations in the acquisition of information from the environment may be hampering the adaptive capacities of the older adult or indeed may be a component of the "intelligence system" itself. Still further explorations in the psychophysiological direction might enable us to correlate the characteristics of the electroencephalogram, sensory evoked potentials, and contingent negative variation in individual differences in set and attention. We could be on the verge of being able to identify specific physiological correlates in the brain with individual differences in intellectual level. Such evidence would help a great deal in separating reversible functional states of the brain from the more irreversible consequences of brain damage.

There have been dramatic changes in many aspects of our society and that of other countries. For example, the educational level has dramatically risen in this century. While there is a high proportion of individuals over the age of 65 who are functionally illiterate, there are not many illiterates of high school age. There are thus large secular trends or cohort differences in the population which ensure that future generations of retired persons will be better educated, and presumably more healthy, than the current generation. What are the upper limits of man's intelligence if potentiated by an environment enriched in information and opportunities of mastering relationships? The consequences of the enriched stream of information that surrounds the average child of today should result in his entering adult life with a greater store of information and possibly a greater capacity for dealing with this information than possessed by present adults.

Many studies still need to be conducted on cohort differences in our intellectual capacities. While the longitudinal study is valuable, it does not inform us about the generational differences resulting from varied experiences, opportunities, or misfortunes. One must attend to the consequences of those significant human experiences associated with war, depression, and natural catastrophies, such as floods and earthquakes. Also, one should be sensitive to the possibilities of strong influences of being reared in an area that is economically and culturally constricting or one that is experiencing a financial and cultural renaissance.

It has been mentioned from time to time that there is a depression mentality associated with being conditioned by the fear of loss. Because of a fear of making mistakes, people afflicted with this type of mentality restrict themselves from exercising creativity and from expanding emotionally. In such cases and others, decision theory and game theory can play a potential role in our studies of the changes in the intellect over the life span. Are there trends within the individual life span whereby early life gains are impressive while in late life losses become dominant? Is an older individual more afraid of making a mistake than of achieving something outstanding and securing rewards? The confident person may overbet with the expectation that he or she will always win whereas the cautious person will under-bet. What are the cohort differences in behavior associated with such adaptive negotiations with life? Such differences in experience may influence how the intellect will be employed or deployed.

Psychology, along with other sciences, is often criticized for dealing with minutia that contain little of significance for the lives of men. Certainly that criticism could not be directed at the subject matter of this book, which indicates that considerable progress has been made and that we can feel confident that this field of endeavor will contribute much to our culture as well as to general psychology. It is important material that will help refine man's concept of his own nature and indeed of his own destiny. It is, however, a field not likely to produce sudden insights, since the nature of the data requires that facts be collected slowly. Also, the interpretation of data will proceed slowly since theory is not tightly articulated. The length of time required to conduct investigations on psychological development and aging suggests that we should soon attempt to make innovative moves to improve the efficiency of our data collecting. It would seem likely that we will see some national samples drawn on a rigorous sampling basis. The issues of development and aging of the intellect are at least as important as some of the topics to which rigorously sampled populations are devoted in surveys. In addition to the carefully sampled national studies, experiments in which crucial variables are manipulated should soon appear: If we really believe we have identified the important independent variable that determines the rate of development or aging of the intellect, then we might attempt to reverse it. For example, the relatively dynamic research area of operant conditioning of somatic responses may afford us the opportunity of modifying brain states to determine their significance for behavior and subsequently, perhaps, to minimize deficits. Conditioning of blood pressure and the alpha wave of the EEG are such examples. It also seems likely that pharmaceutical advances will bring drugs that will influence memory, attention, and perhaps other psychophysiological processes. Psychologists, in turn, must be prepared with valid and reliable measurements of intellectual function to evaluate these drugs.

The papers in this volume suggest that we train our investigators to be sensitive to the methological developments in the social as well as the biological sciences. Whether this can be done appropriately in training individuals or whether it will be necessary to assemble teams of investigators is not clear at this time. The demands of the tasks facing us do require breaking down disciplinary walls to encompass the interrelatedness of psychological, biological, and social influences on aging and human development as exemplified by this volume.

References

Ádám, G. *Interoception and behavior.* Budapest: Akadémiai Kaidó, 1967.

Allport, G. W. *Pattern and growth in personality.* New York: Holt, Rinehart and Winston, 1961.

Andrew, W. Structural alterations with aging in the nervous system. *Journal of Chronic Disease*, 1956, *3*, 575–596.

Apter, N. S., Halstead, W. C., and Heimburger, R. F. Impaired cerebral functions in essential hypertension. *American Journal of Psychiatry*, 1951, *107*, 808–813.

Arenberg, D. Anticipation interval and age differences in verbal learning. *Journal of Abnormal Psychology*, 1965, *70*, 419–425.

Baltes, P. B., Schaie, K. W., and Nardi, A. H. Age and experimental mortality in a seven-year longitudinal study of cognitive behavior. *Developmental Psychology*, 1971, *5*, 18–26.

Bankler, R. G. A correlative study of psychological and EEG findings in normal, physically ill and mentally seniles. *Electroencephalography and Clinical Neurophysiology*, 1967, *22*, 189–190. (Abstract)

Bauer, H. G., Apfeldorf, M. and Hoch, H. Relationship between alpha frequency, age, disease, and intelligence. *Proceedings of the 7th International Congress of Gerontology, Volume 2.* Vienna: Verlag der Wiener Medizinischen Akademie, 1966. pp. 341–349.

Bayley, N. Consistency and variability in the growth of intelligence from birth to eighteen years. *Journal of Genetic Psychology*, 1949, *75*, 165–196.

Bayley, N. The life span as a frame of reference in psychological research. *Vita Humana*, 1963, *6*, 125–139.

Bayley, N. Learning in adulthood: The role of intelligence. In H. J. Klausmeier and

C. W. Harries (Eds.), *Analysis of concept learning*. New York: Academic Press, 1966. pp. 117–138.

Bayley, N. Behavioral correlates of mental growth: Birth to thirty-six years. *American Psychologist*, 1968a, *23*, 1–17.

Bayley, N. Cognition and aging. In K. W. Schaie (Ed.), *Theory and methods of research on aging*. Morgantown, W. Va.: West Virginia University, 1968b. pp. 97–119.

Bayley, N. and Oden, M. H. The maintenance of intellectual ability in gifted adults. *Journal of Gerontology*, 1955, *10*, 91–107.

Bell, A. and Zubek, J. P. The effect of age on the intellectual performance of mental defectives. *Journal of Gerontology*, 1960, *15*, 285–295.

Bennett, R. G. Distinguishing characteristics of the aging from a sociological viewpoint. *Journal of the Americal Geriatrics Society*, 1968, *16*, 127–135.

Bennett, R. G. and Nahemow, L. The relations between social isolation, socialization and adjustment in residents of a home for aged. In M. P. Lawton and F. G. Lawton (Eds.), *Mental impairment in the aged*. Philadelphia: Philadelphia Geriatric Center, 1965. pp. 88–105.

Berkowitz, B. and Green, R. F. Changes in intellect with age: 1. Longitudinal study of Wechsler-Bellevue scores. *Journal of Genetic Psychology*, 1963, *103*, 3–21.

Bettner, L. G., Jarvik, L. F. and Blum, J. E. Stroop color-word test, non-psychotic organic brain syndrome, and chromosome loss in aged twins. *Journal of Gerontology*, 1971, *26*, 458–469.

Birren, J. E. Neural basis of personal adjustment in aging. In P. F. Hansen (Ed.), *Age with a future*. Copenhagen: Munksgaard, 1964. pp. 48–59.

Birren, J. E. Age changes in speed of behavior: Its central nature and physiological correlates. In A. T. Welford and J. E. Birren (Eds.), *Behavior, aging, and the nervous system*. Springfield, Ill.: Charles C. Thomas, 1965. pp. 191–216.

Birren, J. E. Psychological aspects of aging: Intellectual functioning. *The Gerontologist*, 1968, *8*, 16–19.

Birren, J. E. Toward an experimental psychology of aging. *American Psychologist*, 1970, *25*, 124–135.

Birren, J. E., Butler, R. N., Greenhouse, S. W., Sokoloff, L. and Yarrow, M. R. Interdisciplinary relationships: Interrelations of physiological, psychological, and psychiatric findings in healthy elderly men. In J. E. Birren, R. N. Butler, S. W. Greenhouse, L. Sokoloff and M. R. Yarrow (Eds.), *Human aging: A biological and behavioral study*. Washington, D. C.: U. S. Government Printing Office, Public Health Service Publication No. 986, 1963. pp. 283–305.

Birren, J. E. and Morrison, D. F. Analysis of the WAIS subtests in relation to age and education. *Journal of Gerontology*, 1961, *16*, 363–369.

Birren, J. E. and Spieth, W. Age, response speed and cardiovascular functions.

Journal of Gerontology, 1962, *17*, 390–391.

Bleuler, E. *Dementia praecox or the group of schizophrenias.* New York: International University Press, 1950. pp. 266–267.

Block, J. *The Q-sort method in personality assessment and psychiatric research.* Springfield, Ill.: Charles C. Thomas, 1961.

Blum, J. E. Psychological changes between the seventh and ninth decades of life. Doctoral dissertation, St. John's University, 1969.

Blum, J. E., Jarvik, L. F. and Clark, E. T. Rate of change on selective tests of intelligence: A twenty-year longitudinal study of aging. *Journal of Gerontology*, 1970, *25*, 171–176.

Botár, G. *The autonomic nervous system: An introduction to its physiological and pathological histology.* Budapest: Akadémiai Kiadó, 1966.

Botwinick, J. and Birren, J. E. Mental abilities and psychomotor responses in healthy aged men. In J. E. Birren, R. N. Butler, S. W. Greenhouse, L. Sokoloff and M. R. Yarrow (Eds.), *Human aging: A biological and behavioral study.* Washington, D. C.: U.S. Government Printing Office, Public Health Service Publication No. 986, 1963. pp. 97–108.

Botwinick, J. and Kornetsky, C. Age differences in the acquisition and extinction of the GSR. *Journal of Gerontology*, 1960, *15*, 83–84.

Bradburn, N. M. and Caplovitz, D. *Reports on happiness: A pilot study of behavior related to mental health.* Chicago: Aldine Pub. Co., 1965.

Braunwald, E., Epstein, S. E., Glick, G., Wechsler, A. S. and Braunwald, N. Relief of angina pectoris by electrical stimulation of the carotid sinus nerves. *New England Journal of Medicine*, 1967, *277*, 1278–1283.

Briar, S. and Bieri, J. A factor analytic and trait inference study of the Leary Interpersonal Checklist. *Journal of Clinical Psychology*, 1963, *19*, 193–198.

Brodman, K., Erdman, A., Lorge, I., Wolff, H. and Broadbent, T. The Cornell Medical Index: An adjunct to medical interview. *Journal of the American Medical Association*, 1949, *140*, 530–534.

Bühler, C. *Der menschliche lebenslauf als psychologisches problem.* Göttinger, Germany: Verlag für Psychologie, 1959.

Burgess, E. W., Locke, H. J. and Thomas, M. M. *The family from institution to companionship.* New York: American Book Co., 1963. Third Edition.

Busse, E. W. Research on aging: Some methods and finings. In M. A. Berezin and S. H. Cath (Eds.), *Geriatric psychiatry: Grief, loss and emotional disorders in the aging process.* New York: International University Press, 1965. pp. 73–95.

Busse, E. W., Barnes, R. H., Friedman, E. L. and Kelty, E. J. Psychological functioning of aged individuals with normal and abnormal electroencephalograms. 1. A study of non-hospitalized community volunteers. *Journal of Nervous and Mental Diseases*, 1956, *124*, 135–141.

Busse, E. W. and Obrist, W. D. Pre-senescent electroencephalographic changes in normal subjects. *Journal of Gerontology*, 1965, *20*, 315–320.

Busse, E. W. and Wang, H. S. The value of electroencephalography in geriatrics. *Geriatrics*, 1965, *20*, 906–924.

Butler, R. N., Dastur, D. K. and Perlin, S. Relationships of senile manifestations and chronic brain syndromes to cerebral circulation and metabolism. *Journal of Psychiatric Research*, 1965, *3*, 229–238.

Cabanac, M. and Duclaux, R. Obesity: Absence of satiety and aversion to sucrose. *Science*, 1970, *168*, 496–497.

Callaway, E. Response speed, the EEG alpha cycle, and the autonomic cardiovascular cycle. In A.T. Welford and J. E. Birren (Eds.), *Behavior, aging, and the nervous system*. Springfield, Ill.: Charles C. Thomas, 1965. pp. 217–234.

Canestrari, R. E., Jr. Paced and self paced learning in young and elderly adults. *Journal of Gerontology*, 1963, *18*, 165–168.

Cannon, W. B. *Bodily changes in pain, hunger, fear and rage*. Boston: Branford, 1953.

Cohen, B. H. Family patterns of mortality and life span. *Quarterly Review of Biology*, 1964, *39*, 130–181.

Cooley, W. W. and Lohnes, P. R. *Multivariate procedures for the behavioral sciences*. New York: John Wiley, 1962.

Corsellis, J. A. N. *Mental illness and the aging brain*. London: Oxford University Press, 1962. pp. 1–76.

Cronbach, L. J. and Gleser, G. C. Assessing similarity between profiles. *Psychological Bulletin*, 1953, *50*, 456–473.

Dahlstrom, W. and Welsh, G. *An MMPI handbook: A guide to use in clinical practice and research*. Minneapolis: University of Minnesota Press, 1960.

Dailey, C. A. The life history approach to assessment. *Personnel and Guidance Journal*, 1958, *36*, 456–460.

Darrow, C. W. Differences in the physiological reactions to sensory and ideational stimuli. *Psychological Bulletin*, 1929a, *26*, 185–201.

Darrow, C. W. Electrical and circulatory responses to brief sensory and ideational stimuli. *Journal of Experimental Psychology*, 1929b, *12*, 267–300.

Dastur, D. K., Lane, M. H., Hansen, D. B., Kety, S. S., Butler, R. N., Perlin, S., and Sokoloff, L. Effects of aging on cerebral circulation and metabolism in man. In J. E. Birren, R. N. Butler, S. W. Greenhouse, L. Sokoloff and M. R. Yarrow (Eds.), *Human aging: A biological and behavioral study*. Washington, D. C.: U. S. Government Printing Office, Public Health Service Publication No. 986, 1963. pp. 59–76.

Davis, R. C. Response patterns. *Transactions of the New York Academy of Sciences*, 1957, *19*, 731–739.

Dawber, T. R., Kannel, W. B., Revotskie, N., Stokes, J., Kagan, A. and Gordon, T.

Some factors associated with the development of coronary heart disease. Six years follow-up experiment in the Framingham study. *American Journal of Public Health*, 1959, *49*, 1349–1356.

De Carlo, T. J. Recreation participation patterns in successful aging: A twin study. Unpublished Ed. D. thesis, Teachers College, Columbia University, 1971.

Dickens, C. *Martin Chuzzlewit*. Penguin English Library, 1968. pp. 370, 862, and 915.

Donahue, W. Learning, motivation and education of the aging. In J. E. Anderson (Ed.), *Psychological aspects of aging*. Washington, D. C.: American Psychological Association, 1956. pp. 200–206.

Doppelt, J. E. and Wallace, W. L. Standardization of the Wechsler Adult Intelligence Scale for older persons. *Journal of Abnormal and Social Psychology*, 1955, *51*, 312–330.

Ebert, E. and Simmons, K. The Brush Foundation study of child growth and development. 1. Psychometric tests. *Monographs of the Society for Research in Child Development*, 1943, *8* (2, Whole No. 35).

Eisdorfer, C. The WAIS performance of the aged: A retest evaluation. *Journal of Gerontology*, 1963, *18*, 169–172.

Eisdorfer, C. Verbal learning and response time in the aged. *Journal of Genetic Psychology*, 1965, *107*, 15–22.

Eisdorfer, C. Psychologic reaction to cardiovascular change in the aged. *Mayo Clinic Proceedings*, 1967, *42*, 620–636.

Eisdorfer, C. Intellectual changes with advancing age: A 10 year follow-up of the Duke sample. Paper presented at the symposium on "Longitudinal changes with advancing age." American Psychological Association, San Francisco, August-September 1968.

Eisdorfer, C., Busse, E. W., and Cohen, L. D. The WAIS performance of an aged sample: The relationship between verbal and performance I.Q.'s. *Journal of Gerontology*, 1959, *14*, 197–201.

Eisdorfer, C. and Cohen, L. D. The generality of the WAIS standardization for the aged: A regional comparison. *Journal of Abnormal and Social Psychology*, 1961 *62*, 520–527.

Eisdorfer, C., Nowlin, J. and Wilkie, F. Improvement in the aged by modification of autonomic nervous system activity. *Science*, 1970, *170*, 1327–1329.

Ellingson, R. J. Brain waves and problems of psychology *Psychological Bulletin*, 1956, *53*, 1–34.

Engel, B. T. and Hansen, S. P. Operant conditioning of heart rate slowing. *Psychophysiology*, 1966, *3*, 176–187.

Enzer, N., Simonson, E. and Blankstein, S. S. Fatigue of patients with circulatory insufficiency, investigated by means of the fusion frequency of flicker. *Annals of Internal Medicine*, 1942, *16*, 701–707.

Erba, G. and Lombroso, C. T. Detection of ventricular landmarks by two dimensional ultrasonography. *Journal of Neurology, Neurosurgery and Psychiatry*, 1968, *31*, 232-244.

Ermentini, A. and Marinato, G. Correlazioni tra attivita bioelettrica cerebrale ed efficienza intellettiva in un gruppo di anziani. *Giornale di Gerontologia*, 1960, *8*, 1179-1189.

Falek, A., Kallmann, F. J., Lorge, I. and Jarvik, L. F. Longevity and intellectual variation in a senescent twin population. *Journal of Gerontology*, 1960, *15*, 305-309.

Fazekas, J. F. and Alman, R. W. Maximal dilation of cerebral vessels. *Archives of Neurology*, 1964, *11*, 303-309.

Fehr, F. S. Heart rate and behavior of immunosympathectomized rats. (Doctoral dissertation) Ann Arbor, Mich.: University Microfilms, 1966. No. 66-7514.

Feingold, L. A psychometric study of senescent twins. Unpublished doctoral dissertation, Columbia University, 1950.

Folkow, B., Heymans, C. and Neil, E. Integrated aspects of cardiovascular regulation. In W. F. Hamilton and P. Dow (Eds.), *Handbook of physiology: circulation, Volume 111 (Section 2)*. Baltimore: Waverly, 1965. pp. 1787-1823.

Foulds, G. A. and Raven, J. C. Normal changes in the mental abilities of adults as age advances. *Journal of Mental Science*, 1948, *94*, 133-142.

Frolkis, V. V. Neuro-humoral regulations in the aging organism. *Journal of Gerontology*, 1966, *21*, 161-167.

Garg, A. G. and Taylor, A. R. A-scan echoencephalography in measurement of the cerebral ventricles. *Journal of Neurology, Neurosurgery and Psychiatry*, 1968, *31*, 245-249.

Geer, J. H. Measurement of the conditioned cardiac response. *Journal of Comparative and Physiological Psychology*, 1964, *57*, 426-433.

Gilbert, J. G. Mental efficiency in senescene. *Archives of Psychology*, 1935, *27* (Whole No. 188).

Gilmer, R. S. A factorial approach to the life history correlates of intellectual change. Unpublished doctoral dissertation, Purdue University, 1963.

Giovacchini, P. L. and Muslim, H. Ego equilibrium and cancer of the breast. *Psychosomatic Medicine*, 1965, *27*, 524-532.

Gitman, L. (Ed.) *Endocrines and aging*. Springfield, Ill.: Charles C. Thomas, 1967.

Goldfarb, A. I. Predicting mortality in institutionalized aged: A seven-year follow-up. *Archives of General Psychiatry*, 1969, *21*, 172-176.

Goldfarb, A. I., Fisch, M. and Gerber, I. E. Predictors of mortality in the institutionalized aged. *Diseases of the Nervous System*, 1966, *27*, 21-29.

Goldstein, K. *Human nature in the light of psychopathology*. New York: Schocken Books, 1963.

Gosling, R. H. The association of dementia with radiologically demonstrated cerebral atrophy. *Journal of Neurology, Neurosurgery and Psychiatry,* 1955, *18,* 129–133.

Gover, M. Physical impairments of members of low-income farm families—11,490 persons in 2,477 rural families examined by the Farm Security Administration, 1940. VII. Variation of blood pressure and heart disease with age; and the correlation of blood pressure with height and weight. *Public Health Reports,* 1948, *63,* 1083–1101.

Graham, F. K. and Clifton, R. K. Heart-rate change as a component of the orienting response. *Psychological Bulletin,* 1966, *65,* 305–320.

Granick, S. and Birren, J. E. Cognitive functioning of survivors versus non-survivors: A twelve-year follow-up of healthy aged. Paper presented at the Eighth International Congress of Gerontology, Washington, D. C., August 1969 (mimeograph).

Granick, S. and Friedman, A. S. Residual capacities in aged subjects. Paper presented at the annual meeting of the American Psychological Association, Division 20, New York City, September 1966 (mimeograph).

Granick, S. and Friedman, A. S. The effect of education on the decline of psychometric performance with age. *Journal of Gerontology,* 1967, *22,* 191–195.

Granick, R. and Nahemow, L. Preadmission isolation as a factor in adjustment to an old age home. In P. Hock and J. Zubin (Eds.), *Psychopathology of aging.* New York: Grune and Stratton, 1961. pp. 285–302.

Grünthal, E. Die pathologische Anatomie der senilen Demenz und der alzheimerschen Krankheit. In O. Bumke (Ed.), *Handbuch der Geisteskrankheiten, Volume 7.* Berlin: J. Springer, 1930. pp. 638–672.

Guilford, J. P. *Psychometric methods.* New York: McGraw-Hill, 1954.

Guilford, J. P. *The nature of human intelligence.* New York: McGraw-Hill, 1967.

Gutman, D. L. An exploration of ego configurations in middle and later life. In B. L. Neugarten and Associates, *Personality in middle and late life.* New York: Atherton Press, 1964. pp. 114–148.

Haan, N. Proposed model of ego functioning: Coping and defense mechanisms in relation to I.Q. change. *Psychological Monographs,* 1963, *77* (8, Whole No. 571).

Hagnell, O. The premorbid personality of persons who develop cancer in a total population investigated in 1947 and 1957. *Annals of the New York Academy of Sciences,* 1966, *125,* 816–855.

Harman, H. H. *Modern factor analysis.* Chicago: University of Chicago Press, 1960.

Hartman, F. A. and Brownell, K. A. *The adrenal gland.* Philadelphia: Lea and Febiger, 1949.

Harvald, B. EEG in old age. *Acta Psychiatrica et Neurologica Scandinavica,* 1958, *33,* 193–196.

Haug, J. O. Pneumoencephalographic studies in mental disease. *Acta Psychiatrica Scandinavica*, 1962, *38 (Supplementum 165)*, 1–104.

Hedlund, S., Köhler, V., Nylin, G., Olsson, R., Regnström, O. Rothström, E. and Astöm, K. E. Cerebral blood circulation in dementia. *Acta Psychiatrica Scandinavica*, 1964, *40*, 77–106.

Hess, W. R. *The functional organization of the diencephalon.* New York: Grune and Stratton, 1957.

Heyman, D. K. and Jeffers, F. C. Study of relative influences of race and socioeconomic status upon the activities and attitudes of a Southern aged population. *Journal of Gerontology*, 1964, *19*, 225–229.

Heymans, C. and Neil, E. *Reflexogenic areas of the cardiovascular system.* London: Churchill, 1958.

Hillyard, S. A. The CNV and the vertex evoked potential during signal detection: A preliminary report. In E. Donchin and D. B. Lindsley (Eds.), *Average evoked potentials—Methods, results and evaluations.* Washington, D. C.: NASA SP-191, 1969. pp. 349–353.

Hillyard, S. A. and Galambos, R. Effects of stimulus and response contingencies on a surface negative slow potential shift in man. *Electroencephalography and Clinical Neurophysiology*, 1967, *22*, 297–304.

Hoagland, H. Studies of brain metabolism and electrical activity in relation to adrenocortical physiology. In G. Pincus (Ed.), *Recent progress in hormone research, Volume 10.* New York: Academic Press, 1954. pp. 29–63.

Hohmann, G. W. Some effects of spinal cord lesions on experienced emotional feelings. *Psychophysiology*, 1966, *3*, 143–156.

Honzik, M. P. Developmental studies of parent-child resemblance in intelligence. *Child Development*, 1957, *28*, 215–228.

Honzik, M. P. A sex difference in the age of onset of the parent-child resemblance in intelligence. *Journal of Educational Psychology*, 1963, *54*, 231–237.

Honzik, M. P. Environmental correlates of mental growth: Prediction from the family setting at 21 months. *Child Development*, 1967a, *38*, 337–364.

Honzik, M. P. Prediction of differential abilities at age 18 from the early family environment. *Proceedings of the 75th Annual Convention of the American Psychological Association*, 1967b. pp. 151–152.

Honzik, M. P., Macfarlane, J. W., and Allen, L. The stability of mental test performance between two and eighteen years. *Journal of Experimental Education*, 1948, *17*, 309–324.

Ingram, I. M. EEG slowing and intellectual deterioration in the elderly. *Proceedings of the 7th International Congress of Gerontology, Volume 1.* Vienna: Verlag der Wiener Medizinischen Akademie, 1966. pp. 347–350.

Ingvar, D. H., Baldy-Moulinier, M., Sulg, I. and Hormon, S. Regional cerebral blood flow related to EEG. *Acta Neurologica Scandinavica,* 1965, *(Supplementum 14),* 179–182.

Ingvar, D. H. and Risberg, J. Influence of mental activity upon regional cerebral blood flow in man. *Acta Neurologica Scandinavica,* 1965, *(Supplementum 14),* 183–186.

Irwin, D. A., Knott, J. R., McAdam, D. W. and Rebert, C. S. Motivational determinants of the "contingent negative variation." *Electroencephalography and Clinical Neurophysiology,* 1966, *21,* 538–543.

Jalavisto, E. Inheritance of longevity according to Finnish and Swedish genealogies. *Annales Medicinae Internae Fenniae,* 1951, *40,* 263–274.

Jarvik, L. F. Biological differences in intellectual functioning. *Vita Humana,* 1962, *5,* 195–203.

Jarvik, L. F. Survival and psychological aspects of aging in man. *Symposium of the Society for Experimental Biology,* 1967, *21,* 463–482.

Jarvik, L. F. Human genetics and aging. In F. C. Jeffers (Ed.), *Duke University council on aging and human development. Proceedings of seminars. 1965-1969.* Durham, N. C.: Duke University Medical Center, 1969. pp. 266–278.

Jarvik, L. F. and Blum, J. E. Cognitive declines as predictors of mortality in twin pairs: A twenty-year longitudinal study of aging. In E. Palmore and F. C. Jeffers (Eds.), *Prediction of life span.* Lexington, Massachusetts: D. C. Heath, 1971. pp. 199–211.

Jarvik, L. F., Blum, J. E. and Varma, A. O. Genetic components and intellectual functioning during senescence: A twenty-year study of aging twins. *Behavior Genetics,* in press.

Jarvik, L. F. and Erlenmeyer-Kimling, L. Survey of familial correlations in measured intellectual functions. In J. Zubin and G. A. Jervis (Eds.), *Psychopathology of mental development.* New York: Grune and Stratton, 1967. pp. 447–459.

Jarvik, L. F. and Falek, A. Intellectual stability and survival in the aged. *Journal of Gerontology,* 1963, *18,* 173–176.

Jarvik, L. F., Falek, A., Kallmann, F. J. and Lorge, I. Survival trends in a senescent twin population. *American Journal of Human Genetics,* 1960, *12,* 170–179.

Jarvik, L. F., Kallmann, F. and Falek, A. Intellectual changes in aged twins. *Journal of Gerontology,* 1962, *17,* 289–294.

Jarvik, L. F., Kallmann, F. J., Falek, A. and Klaber, M. M. Changing intellectual functions in senescent twins. *Acta Genetica Et Statistica Medica,* 1957, *7,* 421–430.

Jarvik, L. F. and Kato, T. Chromosome examinations in aged twins. *American Journal of Human Genetics,* 1970, *22,* 562–573.

Johnstone, J. W. C. and Rivera, R. J. *Volunteers for learning.* Chicago: Aldine Publishing Co., 1965.

Justiss, W. A. The electroencephalogram of the frontal lobes and abstract behavior in old age. In H. T. Blumenthal (Ed.), *Medical and clinical aspects of aging.* New York: Columbia University Press, 1962. pp. 556–574.

Kallmann, F. J. and Jarvik, L. F. Individual differences in constitution and genetic background. In J. E. Birren (Ed.), *Handbook of aging and the individual: psychological and biological aspects.* Chicago: University of Chicago Press, 1959, pp. 216–263.

Kallmann, F. J. and Sander, G. Twin studies on aging and longevity. *Journal of Heredity,* 1948, *39,* 349–357.

Kallmann, F. J. and Sander, G. Twin studies on senescence. *American Journal of Psychiatry,* 1949, *106,* 29–36.

Kaplan, O. Mental decline in older morons. *American Journal of Mental Deficiency,* 1943, *47,* 277–285.

Kaplan, O. J. *Mental disorders in later life.* Stanford: Standford University Press, 1956.

Kety, S. S. and Schmidt, C. F. The determination of cerebral blood flow in man by the use of nitrous oxide in low concentrations. *American Journal of Physiology,* 1945, *143,* 53–66.

King, H. E. Comparison of fine psychomotor movement by hypertensive and hypotensive subjects. *Perceptual and Motor Skills,* 1956, *6,* 199–204.

Kinsey, A. C., Pomeroy, W. B. and Martin, C. E. *Sexual behavior in the human male.* Philadelphia: W. B. Saunders Co., 1948.

Kinsey, A. C., Pomeroy, W. B., Martin, C. E. and Gebhard, P. H. *Sexual behavior in the human female.* Philadelphia: W. B. Saunders Co., 1953.

Klee, A. The relationship between clinical evaluation of mental deterioration, psychological test results, and the cerebral metabolic rate of oxygen. *Acta Neurologica Scandinavica,* 1964, *40,* 337–345.

Kleemeier, R. W. Intellectual changes in the senium, or death and the I.Q. Presidential address, Division on Maturity and Old Age, American Psychological Association, September 1, 1961.

Kleemeier, R. W. Intellectual change in the senium. *Proceedings of the Social Statistics Section of the American Statistical Association,* 1962, 290–295.

Lacey, B. C. and Lacey, J. I. Cardiovascular and respiratory correlates of reaction time. Appended Preprint No. 3, progress Report, Grant MH–00623, June, 1965.

Lacey, J. I. Psychophysiological approaches to the evaluation of psychotherapeutic process and outcome. In E. A. Rubenstein and M. B. Parloff (Eds,). *Research in psychotherapy.* Washington: National Publishing Co., 1959. pp. 160–208.

Lacey, J. I. Cardiac and cortical activity during the preparatory interval in a reaction time experiment. *American Psychologist,* 1966, *21,* 714 (Abstract).

Lacey, J. I. Somatic response patterning and stress: Some revisions of activation theory. In M. H. Appley and R. Trumbull (Eds.), *Psychological stress: Issues in research*. New York: Appleton Century Crofts, 1967. pp. 14–42.

Lacey, J. I., Kagan, J., Lacey, B. C. and Moss, H. A. The visceral level: Situational determinants and behavioral correlates of autonomic response patterns. In P. H. Knapp (Ed.), *Expression of the emotions in man*. New York: International University Press, 1963. pp. 161–196.

Lacey, J. I. and Lacey, B. C. Psychophysiology of the autonomic nervous system. Progress Report, Grant MH–00623, June, 1965.

Lacey, J. I. and Lacey, B. C. Some autonomic-central nervous system interrelationships. In P. Black (Ed.), *Physiological correlates of emotion*. New York: Academic Press, 1970. pp. 205–227.

Lang, P. J. and Melamed, B. G. Case report: Avoidance conditioning therapy of an infant with chronic ruminative vomiting. *Journal of Abnormal Psychology*, 1969, *74*, 1–8.

Lange, C. G. and James, W. *The emotions*. Baltimore: Williams and Wilkins, 1922.

Langner, T. S. and Michael, S. T. *Life stress and mental health*. New York: Free Press of Glencoe, 1963.

Lassen, N. A., Munck, O. and Tottey, E. R. Mental function and cerebral oxygen consumption in organic dementia. *Archives of Neurology and Psychiatry*, 1957, *77*, 126–133.

Leary, T. The theory and measurement methodology of interpersonal communication. *Psychiatry*, 1955, *18*, 147–161.

Levene, H. I., Engel, B. T. and Pearson, J. A. Differential operant conditioning of heart rate. *Psychosomatic Medicine*, 1968, *30*, 837–845.

Levi-Montalcini, R. and Angeletti, P. U. Nerve growth factor. *Physiological Reviews*, 1968, *48*, 534–569.

Lieberman, M. A. Psychological correlates of impending death: Some preliminary observations. *Journal of Gerontology*, 1965, *20*, 181–190.

Lieberman, M. A. Observations on death and dying. *The Gerontologist*, 1966, *6*, 70–72.

Lorge, I. Capacities of older adults. In W. T. Donahue (Ed.), *Education for later maturity: A handbook*. New York: Whiteside and Morrow, 1955. pp. 36–59.

Low, M. D., Borda, R. P., Frost, J. D., Jr. and Kellaway, P. Surface-negative, slow-potential shift associated with conditioning in man. *Neurology*, 1966, *16*, 771–782.

Maccoby, E. E. *The development of sex differences*. Stanford: Stanford University Press, 1966.

Maddox, G. L. Selected methodological issues. *Proceedings of the Social Statistics Section of the American Statistical Association*, 1962, 280–285.

Marks, H. H. Characteristics and trends of cerebral vascular disease. In P. Hoch and J. Zubin (Eds.), *Psychopathology of aging*. New York: Grune and Stratton, 1961. pp. 69–99.

Master, A. M., Garfield, C. I. and Walters, M. B. *Normal blood pressure and hypertension*. Philadelphia: Lea and Febiger, 1952.

Mednick, S. A. and Schulsinger, F. Some premorbid characteristics related to breakdown in children with schizophrenic mothers. In D. Rosenthal and S. S. Kety (Eds.), *The transmission of schizophrenia*. London: Permagon Press, 1968. pp. 267–291.

Miles, C. C. Influence of speed and age on intelligence scores of adults. *Journal of General Psychology*, 1934, *10*, 208–210.

Miller, N. E. Learning of visceral and glandular responses. *Science*, 1969, *163*, 434–445.

Milner, B. Psychological defects produced by temporal lobe excision. In H. C. Solomon, S. Cobb and W. Penfield (Eds.), *The brain and human behavior* (Research Publications, Association for Research in Nervous and Mental Disease, Vol. 36). Baltimore: Williams and Wilkins Co., 1958. pp. 244–257.

Mirsky, I. A. Psychoanalysis and human behavior: Experimental approaches. In A. D. Bass (Ed.) *Evolution of nervous control from primitive organisms to man*. Publication No. 52, American Association for the Advancement of Science, Washington, D. C., 1959. pp. 195–226.

Mithoefer, J. C. and Karetzky, M. S. The cardiopulmonary system in the aged. In J. H. Powers (Ed.), *Surgery of the aged and debilitated patient*. Philadelphia: W. B. Saunders, 1968. pp. 138–164.

Morin, K., Baer, P. E., Elster, S. H. and McRoberts, A. Towards a life history interview for use with the elderly. Paper presented at the annual meeting of the American Psychological Association, San Francisco, September 1968.

Morris, J. D. and Thompson, L. W. Heart rate changes in a reaction time experiment with young and aged subjects. *Journal of Gerontology*, 1969, *24*, 269–275.

Mundy-Castle, A. C. Central excitability in the aged. In H. T. Blumenthal (Ed.), *Medical and clinical aspects of aging*. New York: Columbia University Press, 1962. pp. 575–595.

Murray, H. A. *Thematic apperception test: Pictures and manual*. Cambridge: Harvard University Press, 1943.

Murray, H. A. Toward a classification of interactions. In T. Parsons and E. Shils (Eds.), *Towards a general theory of action*. Cambridge: Harvard University Press, (1951). 1962. pp. 434–464.

Nelson, R. and Gellhorn, E. The action of autonomic drugs on normal persons and neuropsychiatric patients. *Psychosomatic Medicine*, 1957, *19*, 486–494.

Nelson, R. and Gellhorn, E. The influence of age and functional neuropsychiatric disorders on sympathetic and parasympathetic functions. *Journal of Psychoso-*

matic Research, 1958, *3,* 12–26.

Nielsen, R., Petersen, O., Thygesen, P. and Willanger, R. Encephalographic cortical atrophy: Relationships to ventricular atrophy and intellectual impairment. *Acta Radiologica (Diagnosis),* 1966a, *4,* 437–448.

Nielsen, R., Petersen, O., Thygensen, P. and Willanger, R. Encephalographic ventricular atrophy: Relationships between size of ventricular system and intellectual impairment. *Acta Radiologica (Diagnosis).* 1966b, *4,* 240–256.

Niijima, A. Afferent impulse discharges from glucoreceptors in the liver of the guinea pig. *Annals of the New York Academy of Sciences,*1969, *157,* 690–700.

Niijima, A. and Winter, D. L. Baroreceptors in the adrenal gland. *Science,* 1968a, *159,* 434–435.

Niijima, A. and Winter, D. L. The effect of catecholamines on unit activity in afferent nerves from the adrenal glands. *Journal of Physiology,* 1968b, *195,* 647–656.

Nisbet, J. D. Intelligence and age: Retesting with twenty-four years interval. *British Journal of Educational Psychology,* 1957, *27,* 190–198.

Norries, A. H., Shock, N. W. and Yiengst, M. J. Age changes in heart rate and blood pressure responses to tilting and standardized exercise. *Circulation,* 1953, *8,* 521–526.

Nowlin, J. B., Eisdorfer, C. and Thompson, L. W. Cardiovascular response during reaction time performance. Unpublished manuscript, 1970a.

Nowlin, J. B., Eisdorfer, C. and Thompson, L. W. Effects of age on cardiovascular responses during reaction time performance. Unpublished manuscript, 1970b.

Obrist, P. A. Cardiovascular differentiation of sensory stimuli. *Psychosomatic Medicine,* 1963, *25,* 450–459.

Obrist, W. D. Simple auditory reaction time in aged adults. *Journal of Psychology,* 1953, *35,* 259–266.

Obrist, W. D. Cerebral ischemia and the senescent electroencephalogram. E. Simonson and T. H. McGavack (Eds.), *Cerebral ischemia.* Springfield, Illinois: Charles C. Thomas, 1964. pp. 71–96.

Obrist, W. D. Electroencephalographic approach to age changes in response speed. In A. T. Welford and J. E. Birren (Eds.), *Behavior, aging and the nervous system.* Springfield, Illinois: Charles C. Thomas, 1965. pp. 259–271.

Obrist, W. D., Busse, E. W., Eisdorfer, C. and Kleemeier, R. W. Relation of the electroencephalogram to intellectual function in senescence. *Journal of Gerontology,* 1962, *17,* 197–206.

Obrist, W. D., Busse, E. W. and Henry, C. E. Relation of electroencephalogram to blood pressure in elderly persons. *Neurology,* 1961, *11,* 151–158.

Obrist, W. D., Sokoloff, L., Lassen, N. A., Lane, M. H., Butler, R. N. and Feinberg, I. Relation of EEG to cerebral blood flow and metabolism in old age. *Electroencephalography and Clinical Neurophysiology,* 1963, *15,* 610–619.

Obrist, W. D., Thompson, H. K., King, C. H. and Wang, H. S. Determination of regional cerebral blood flow by inhalation of 133-xenon. *Circulation Research,* 1967, *20,* 124–135.

Obrist, P. A., Webb, R. A., Sutterer, J. R. and Howard, J. L. Cardiac deceleration and reaction time: An evaluation of two hypotheses. *Psychophysiology,* 1970a, *6,* 695–706.

Obrist, P. A., Webb, R. A., Sutterer, J. R. and Howard, J. L. The cardiac-somatic relationship: Some reformulations. *Psychophysiology,* 1970b, *6,* 569–587.

Owens, W. Age and mental abilities: A longitudinal study. *Genetic Psychology Monographs,* 1953, *48,* 3–54.

Owens, W. A., Jr. Is age kinder to the initially more able? In *Proceedings of the Fourth Congress of the International Association of Gerontology.* Fidenza, Italy: Tipographia Tito Mattioli, 1957, *4,* 151–157.

Owens, W. A. Age and mental abilities: A second adult follow-up. *Journal of Educational Psychology,* 1966, *57,* 311–325.

Paintal, A. S. Vagal afferent fibers. *Ergebn-Physiology,* 1963, *52,* 74–156.

Palmore, E. B. Physical, mental and social factors in predicting longevity. *The Gerontologist,* 1969, *9,* 103–108.

Pickering, G. W. *The nature of essential hypertension.* New York: Grune and Stratton, 1961.

Pressey, S. L. Major problems—and the major problem—motivation, learning and education in the later years. In J. E. Anderson (Ed.), *Psychological aspects of aging.* Washington, D. C.: American Psychological Association, 1956. pp. 195–199.

Prosser, C. L. Comparative neurophysiology. In A. D. Bass (Ed.), *Evolution of nervous control from prinitive organisms to man.* Publication No. 52, American Association for the Advancement of Science, Washington, D. C., 1959. pp. 31–42.

Rabourn, R. E. A comparison of the Wechsler Bellevue I and the Wechsler Adult Intelligence Scale. Unpublished manuscript. Counseling Center, University of California, Berkeley, 1957.

Rebert, C. S., McAdam, D. W., Knott, J. R. and Irwin, D. A. Slow potential change in human brain related to level of motivation. *Journal of Comparative and Physiological Psychology,* 1967, *63,* 20–23.

Reed, H. B. and Reitan, R. M. Changes in psychological test performance associated with the normal aging process. *Journal of Gerontology,* 1963, *18,* 271–274.

Reitan, R. M. Intellectual and affective changes in essential hypertension. *American Journal of Psychiatry,* 1954, *110,* 817–824.

Reitan, R. M. Investigation of the validity of Halstead's Measures of Biological Intelligence. *A. M. A. Archives of Neurology and Psychiatry,* 1955, *73,* 28–35.

Riegel, K. F. The northern Germany study. Paper read at the International Congress of Gerontology, Vienna, 1966.

Riegel, K. F. Research designs in the study of aging and the prediction of retest-resistance and death. *Proceedings of the 8th International Congress of Gerontology*, Washington, D. C., 1969. *Vol. 1*. pp. 455–457.

Riegel, K. F., Riegel, R. M. and Meyer, G. A study of the dropout rate in longitudinal research on aging and the prediction of death. *Journal of Personality and Social Psychology*, 1967, *5*, 342–348.

Riese, W. The cerebral cortex in the very old human brain. *Journal of Neuropathology and Experimental Neurology*, 1946, *5*, 160–164.

Riesman, D. Some clinical and cultural aspects of the aging process. In D. Riesman, *Individualism reconsidered*. Glencoe, Illinois: The Free Press, 1954. pp. 484–491.

Rogers, C. R. *Client-centered therapy*. Boston: Houghton Mifflin, 1951.

Roth, M., Tomlinson, B. E. and Blessed, G. The relationship between quantitative measures of dementia and of degenerative changes in the cerebral grey matter of elderly subjects. *Proceedings of the Royal Society of Medicine*, 1967, *60*, 254–258.

Roth, M., Tomlinson, B. and Blessed, G. Quantitative measures of psychological impairment and cerebral damage (at post mortem) in normal and demented elderly subjects with a note on the significance of threshold effects. Paper presented at the 8th International Congress of Gerontology, Washington, D. C., August 1969.

Rothschild, D. Pathological changes in senile psychoses and their psychobiologic significance. *American Journal of Psychiatry*, 1937, *93*, 757–788.

Ruckmick, C. A. *The psychology of feeling and emotion*. New York: McGraw-Hill, 1936.

Rushmer, R. F. and Smith, O. A. Cardiac control. *Physiological Reviews*, 1959, *39*, 41–68.

Sanderson, R. E. and Inglis, J. Learning and mortality in elderly psychiatric patients. *Journal of Gerontology*, 1961, *16*, 375–376.

Schaie, K. W. and Strother, C. R. Cognitive and personality variables in college graduates of advanced age. In G. A. Talland (Ed.), *Human aging and behavior*. New York: Academic Press, 1968a. pp. 281–308.

Schaie, K. W. and Strother, C. R. The effect of time and cohort differences on the interpretation of age changes in cognitive behavior. *Multivariate Behavioral Research*, 1968b, *3*, 259–293.

Schoenfeldt, L. F. Life experience as a moderator in the prediction of educational criteria. Paper presented at meeting of the American Educational Research Association, Minneapolis, March 1970.

Scholander, P. F. Physiological adaptation to diving in animals and man. *Harvey*

Lectures, 1961–62, *57,* 93–110.

Shmavonian, B. M., Yarmat, A. J. and Cohen, S. I. Relationships between the autonomic nervous system and central nervous system in age differences in behavior. In A. T. Welford and J. E. Birren (Eds.), *Behavior, aging and the nervous system.* Springfield, Illinois: Charles C. Thomas, 1965. pp. 235–258.

Silverman, A. J., Busse, E. W., Barnes, R. H., Frost, L. L. and Thaler, M. B. Physiologic influences on psychic functioning in elderly people. *Geriatrics,* 1953, *8,* 370–376.

Sim, M., Turner, E. and Smith, W. T. Cerebral biopsy in the investigation of presenile dementia. 1. Clinical Aspects. *British Journal of Psychiatry,* 1966, *112,* 119–125.

Simon, A. Physical illness and socio-psychologic problems in the aged mentally ill. *Proceedings of the 8th International Congress of Gerontology, Volume 1.* Washington, D. C., 1969. pp. 202–205.

Sontag, L. W., Baker, C. T. and Nelson, V. L. Mental growth and personality development: A longitudinal study. *Monographs of the Society for Research in Child Development,* 1958, *23* (2), Whole No. 68.

Spieth, W. Abnormally slow perceptual-motor task performances in individuals with stable, mild to moderate heart disease. *Aerospace Medicine,* 1962, *33,* 370. (Abstract)

Spieth, W. Cardiovascular health status, age, and psychological performance. *Journal of Gerontology,* 1964, *19,* 277–284.

Spieth, W. Slowness of task performance and cardiovascular diseases. In A. T. Welford and J. E. Birren (Eds.), *Behavior, aging, and the nervous system.* Springfield, Illinois: Charles C. Thomas, 1965. pp. 366–400.

Spitzer, R. L., Endicott, J., Cohen, J. ,Bennett, R. and Weinstock, C. Mental Status Schedule—Geriatric Supplement. Biometrics Research, New York State Department of Mental Hygiene; Research Division, Washington Heights Community Service, New York State Psychiatric Institute; Department of Psychiatry, Columbia University, 1969.

Spitzer, R. L., Fleiss, J. L., Endicott, J. and Cohen, J. Mental status schedule: Properties of factor-analytically derived scales. *Archives of General Psychiatry,* 1967, *16,* 479–493.

Srole, L., Langner, T. S., Michael, S. T., Opler, M. K. and Rennis, T. A. C. *Mental health in the metropolis—the midtown Manhattan study.* New York: McGraw-Hill, 1962. Volume 1.

Starmer, C. F. A multivariate analysis program for biomedical research. *Proceedings of the 6th Annual Southeastern Regional Meeting of the Association for Computing Machinery aand the National Meeting for Biomedical Computing,* June, 1967, *2.*

Talland, G. A. Initiation of response, and reaction time in aging, and with brain damage. In A. T. Welford and J. E. Birren (Eds.), *Behavior, aging, and the nervous system.* Springfield, Illinois: Charles C. Thomas, 1965. pp. 526–561.

Tecce, J. J. and Scheff, N. M. Attention reduction and suppressed direct-current potentials in the human brain. *Science,* 1969, *164,* 331–333.

Thaler, M. Relationships among Wechsler, Weigl, Rorschach, EEG findings, and abstract-concrete behavior in a group of normal aged subjects. *Journal of Gerontology,* 1956, *11,* 404–409.

Thompson, C. W. Decline in limit of performance among adult morons. *American Journal of Psychology,* 1951, *64,* 203–215.

Thompson, L. W., Eisdorfer, C. and Estes, E. H. Cardiovascular disease and behavioral changes in the elderly. In *Proceedings of the 7th International Congress of Gerontology, Volume 1.* Vienna: Verlag der Wiener Medizinischen Akademie, 1966. pp. 387–390.

Thompson, L. W. and Wilson, S. Electrocortical reactivity and learning in the elderly. *Journal of Gerontology,* 1966, *21,* 45–51.

Turton, E. C. The EEG as a diagnostic and prognostic aid in the differentiation of organic disorders in patients over 60. *Journal of Mental Science,* 1958, *104,* 461–465.

U. S. Bureau of the Census. Census of Population, Vol. 1, Part 1, 1960.

U. S. Bureau of the Census. Current Population Reports, P–20, No. 80, 1958.

U. S. Bureau of the Census. Current Population Reports, P–25, No. 305, 1965.

Vogel, W. and Broverman, D. M. Relationship between EEG and test intelligence: A critical review. *Psychological Bulletin,* 1964, *62,* 132–144.

Walter, W. G. Brain responses to semantic stimuli. *Journal of Psychosomatic Research,* 1965, *9,* 51–61.

Walter, W. G. Cooper, R., Aldridge, V. J., McCallum, W. C. and Winter, A. L. Contingent negative variation: An electric sign of sensorimotor association and expectancy in the human brain. *Nature,* 1964, *203,* 380—384.

Wang, H. S., Obrist, W. D. and Busse, E. W. Electroencephalographic and intellectual changes in healthy elderly: A longitudinal study. *The Gerontologist,* 1967, *7,* 23.

Ward, J. H., Jr. Hierarchical grouping to optimize an objective function. *Journal of the American Statistical Association,* 1963, *58,* 236–244.

Ward, J. H., Jr. and Hook, M. E. Application of an hierarchical grouping procedure to a problem of grouping profiles. *Educational and Psychological Measurement,* 1963, *23,* 69–81.

Waszak, M. and Obrist, W. D. Relationship of slow potential changes to response speed and motivation in man. *Electroencephalography and Clinical Neurophysiology,* 1969, *27,* 113–120.

Webber, I. L. The educable aged. In J. C. Dixon (Ed.), *Continuing education in the later years*. Gainesville, Florida: University of Florida Press, 1963. pp. 14–25.

Wechsler, D. *Manual for the Wechsler Adult Intelligence Scale*. New York: Phychological Corporation, 1955.

Wechsler, D. *The measurement and appraisal of adult intelligence*. Baltimore: Williams and Wilkins Company, 1958.

Weinstock, C. and Bennett, R. Relations between social isolation, social cognition and related cognitive skills in the aged. Paper read at Gerontological Society meetings, Denver, 1968. (Revised version in press, *Journal of Aging and Human Development*.)

Weiss, T. and Engel, B. T. Operant conditioning of heart rate in patients with premature ventricular contractions. *Psychosomatic Medicine*, 1971, *33*, 301–321.

Welford, A. T. *Aging and human skill*. London: Oxford University Press, 1958.

Welford, A. T. Performance, biological mechanisms and age: A theoretical sketch. In A. T. Welford and J. E. Birren (Eds.), *Behavior, aging, and the nervous system*. Springfield, Illinois: Charles C. Thomas, 1965. pp. 3–20.

Wilkie, F. and Eisdorfer, C. Intelligence and blood pressure in the aged. *Science*, 1971, *172*, 959–962.

Wilson, R. S. Autonomic changes produced by noxious and innocuous stimulation. *Journal of Comparative and Physiological Psychology*, 1964, *58*, 290–295.

Winer, B. J. *Statistical principles in experimental design*. New York: McGraw-Hill, 1962.

Winter, D. L. and Niijima, A. Baroreceptor reflex mechanisms: Systemic and regional. *Proceedings of the International Federation of Automatic Control Symposium on Technical and Biological Problems of Control*. Yerevan, USSR, 1968.

Wolf, S. G., Cardon, P. V., Shepard, E. M. and Wolff, H. G. *Life, stress and essential hypertension*. Baltimore: Williams and Wilkins, 1955.

Wolff, H. G. *Stress and disease* (2nd ed.). Revised and edited by S. Wolf and H. Goodell. Springfield, Illinois: Charles C. Thomas, 1968.

Wood, D. M. and Obrist, P. A. Minimal and maximal sensory intake and exercise as conditioned stimuli in human heart rate conditioning. Unpublished manuscript, 1966.

Yakovlev, P. I. Anatomy of the human brain and the problem of mental retardation. In P. W. Bowman and H. V. Mautner (Eds.), *Mental Retardation—Proceedings of the First International Medical Conference at Portland, Maine*. New York: Grune and Stratton, 1960. pp. 1–43.

Index

A

Activities and interests, 19, 131, 139
Adaptation process, 150
    to change and stress, 132
    life history interviews, 137–142
Adult development and aging, 137–142
Adult Development Research Program, 1, 138
Affectional interaction, 57
Afferent pathways, 72, 73
Age Center of New England Study, 7–12
Age changes, vi, 2
    effect on mental abilities, 31, 42
    effect on visceral nervous system, 77–88
    life history subgroups and, 31–44
    physical and mental changes, vi See also Intellectual functioning
Alpha tests, 32, 38–40, 66
Alzheimer's disease, 96
American Psychological Association, Division on Adult Development and Aging, v-vi
Angina pectoris, 75
Arithmetic tests, 3, 6, 47
Army Alpha Tests, 32, 38–40, 66
Arteriosclerosis, cerebral, 101
Attention, 154
    contingent negative variation, 117–122, 152
    effect on reaction time performance, 107–123
    relation to nervous system, 107–123

B

Baroreceptors, 73–74
Bayley, Nancy, 47
Behavioral changes
    blood pressure and, 84–93
    goals and strategies, 150
    indicator of physiologic state, 126
    systemic disease and, 83–93
Bennett, Ruth, 127–135, 143–148
Berkeley Growth Study, vi, 1, 47
    ages covered, 1–2

longitudinal study, 1–2
Berkeley Guidance Study, 46–47, 49
    interviews with parents, 49
    personality development, 49
    sample, 46
Bettner, Louise, vii
Birren, James E., 149–154
Block Design tests, 3
Blood flow and intelligence, 101–104
Blood pressure and intelligence, 70, 73–74, 83–93
    effect on intellectual functioning, vi, 83–93
    examination procedures, 85–86
    heart rate changes and, 111–116
    method, 85
    results, 86–90
    summary and discussion, 90–93
    ten-year follow-up study, 92–93
    WAIS scores and, 88–92
Blum, June E., 13–20, 146
Blumner, B., 127–135
Body and mind, 69–82, 125–127
    central nervous system, 69–72
    environmental influences, 125–127
    findings in aging organism, 77–88
    function of nervous system, 72, 74–77
    mechanism of interaction, 69–82
    receptors and reflexes, 72–73
    social influences, 125–127
    visceral nervous system, 72, 77–88
Brain status and intelligence, 69–82, 95–105
    biopsy studies, 95–96
    cerebral blood flow studies, 101–104
    cerebral correlates of intellectual functioning, 95–105
    contingent negative variation, 152
    current concepts, 70–72
    Duke Longitudinal Project, 95–105
    electroencephalographic studies, 97–101
    histopathological studies, 95–96
    intellectual function and, 95–105
    pneumoencephalographic studies, 97
    research in modifying brain states, 154
    senile changes, 95–97

C

California Preschool Scales, 46
Cardiovascular disease, destructive influence, 66, 70, 73–74, 83–93
Casals, Pablo, 62
Cerebral correlates of intellectual functioning, 95–105
  blood flow studies, 101–104
  Duke Longitudinal Project, 98–100, 102–104
  EEG abnormalities, 97–98
  histopathological studies, 95–96
Chronological age and psychological functioning, 19
Clark, Edward T., 13–20
Cognitive decline, 66–67
Cohen, Donna, vii
Comprehension tests, 3
Contingent negative variation, 117–122, 152
  age differences, 117, 121, 123
Cornell Medical Index, 8, 12
Coronary heart disease, 83
Creative output, 61
"Critical loss" concept, 15–17
Cross-sectional studies, 31, 84–85
  Duke Longitudinal Project, 22, 25–26
  intellectual functioning, 8
  life history interview schedule, 146
Culture, attitudes toward aging, 59–60, 67
Current History Questionnaire, 8
Cytogenetics, 19

D

Debilitating aspects of aging, 59–60
Decision theory, 153
Dementia, presenile, 96–97
Descartes, René, 69–70
Deterioration with advancing age, 59–60, 67, 91
Developmental process, 149–150
Dickens, Charles, 70
Digit Span tests, 3, 47
Digit Symbol speed test, 3, 6, 47, 57
Drugs, to modify brain states, 154
Duke Longitudinal Research Project, 21–29
  blood pressure and intelligence study, 83–93
  brain status and intelligence, 95–105
  cerebral blood flow studies, 101–104

Duke Longitudinal Research Project (*cont.*)
  conclusions, 27–29
  cross-sectional analysis, 22, 25–26
  EEG studies, 98–100
  effect of age on intellectual functioning, 21
  four examinations, 22
  intellectual changes over time, 22–23, 26–27
  initial level of intelligence and decline in intellectual performance, 21, 28
  methods and sample, 22–23
  Non-Survivors Group, 22
  results, 23–27
  Survivors Group, 22
  ten-year study, 21–29
  WAIS scores, 23–29
Duke University Center for the Study of Aging and Human Development, 22, 85, 105

E

Education for the aged, 63, 152–153
  adult education opportunities, 61–64
  intellectual functioning and, 59–64
  learning and memory experiments, 61
  level of education, 62
  motivation, 62–63
  research investigations, 59–63
  stimulus to intellectual capacities, 63
Eichorn, Dorothy H., 1–6, 66
Eisdorfer, Carl, 21–29, 66, 83–93, 125–126, 146
Electroencephalographic (EEG) studies, 97–101
  focal disturbances, 97–98
Emotional feelings, 70
Epinephrine, effects of, 72, 73

F

Familial variables, 132, 140
Friedman, Alfred S., 59, 66

G

Game theory, 153
Goals and aspiration, 139–140, 150
  life-span changes, 142
Gordon, Chad, 7–12, 66, 146
Granick, Samuel, 59, 66
Grouping techniques, 33–42
  clustering similar profiles, 33–34

hierarchical procedures, 43–44
identification of misfits, 34
life history profiles, 43

H

Halstead Impairment Index, 83
Health and medication, 130–131
Health status changes, 12, 19
hypertension and intelligence, 83–93
intellectual functioning and, 61, 126, 151
key factor, 66
life history interviews, 139
systemic disease and behavioral correlates, 83–93
Heart rate
attention and changes in, 108–111
reaction time changes and, 108–111
Hereditary aspects, 14
Honzik, Marjorie P., 45–58, 66
Hypertension and intelligence, 73, 83–93

I

Information tests, 3
Institute of Human Development Studies, 1–6
Berkeley Growth Study, vi, 1–2, 46–47
Berkeley Guidance Study, 1–2, 46–47, 49
Oakland Growth Study, 1, 2
Intelligence Quotient, *see* IQ
Intellectual functioning
brain changes and, 95–105
cerebral correlates in senescence, 95–105
changes over life span, 1–6, 153
cross-sectional studies, 8
decline in speeded motor tasks, 65–66
different patterns of intellectual growth, 1–6, 53–56
different rates of intellectual decline, 22, 28
educational experience and, 59–64, 66
effect of age changes and, 21, 31, 42
effect of blood pressure on, vi, 70, 73–74, 83–93
gains and losses in IQ over 22 year period, 47–49
health status and, 126, 151
increase in, 7
individual differences, 1–6, 150–151
initial level of intelligence and decline in, 21
longitudinal tests, 1–6, 7–12

patterns of, 65–67
personality development and, 45–58
predicting, 45–46
prospects and problems of research, 149–154
sex differences, 2–3
stability of, 65–66
subnormal abilities, 28
superior abilities, 28
test-retest performance, 8–10
IQ
different patterns of intellectual growth, 53–56
gains and losses over 22-year period, 47–49
personality characteristics and, 49–53
of subject's children, 48
Iowa State University, 32

J

Jarvik, Lissy F., 13–20, 65–67, 127–135, 146, 147

L

Learning, capacity for, 60–61
Leary Interpersonal Checklist, 8, 10–12
Life Experience Inventory, 32
Life experiences
assimilation and accommodation, 53
mental abilities and, 31–44
Life history interview schedules, 19, 32–44, 127–135
activities and interests, 139
adult development study and, 137–142
biomedical aspects, 130–131
and changes in mental abilities, 31–44
core questionnaires, 147
cross-sectional studies, 146
description of, 130–135
data gathering techniques, 147–148
design of, 127–135, 138–139
evaluation of life course, 140–141
family orientation, 140
goals and aspirations, 139–140
guidelines for, 146
health history, 139
intelligence tests, 141
lack of adequate information, vi, 143–148
personality characteristics, 142
psychiatric symptoms, 139
psychological aspects, 132–134

reliability and validity of items, 147
research design, 127–130, 138–139
    need for longitudinal research, 143–148
    prospects and problems, 151
    self-reports, 147
    social relationships, 141–142, 147
    sociological aspects, 131, 139
    subgroups as moderators, 32–44
Life stresses, 132
Longevity, 128–129
    hereditary aspects, 14
    need for longitudinal research, 148
Longitudinal research, vi, 2, 31
    Age Center of New England study, 7–12
    cohort differences, 153
    Duke Project, 21–29
    individual changes in adult intelligence,
        1–6
    life history subgroups, 31–44
    personality and intelligence, 45–58
    prospects and problems, 149–154
    psychological studies of age differences,
        31–44
    study of aging twins, 13–20
Loss, fear of, 153

M

Macfarlane, Jean W., 45–58, 66
Memory, 154
    experiments, 61
Mental abilities, 19
    effect of blood flow, 101–104
    increments in, 2
Mental abilities
    life experience and, 31–44
    See also Intellectual functioning
Mental breakdowns, 132
Mind and body *see* Body and mind; Brain
    status and intelligence
Minnesota Multiphasic Personality Inven-
    tory (MMPI), 8, 10–12
Mistakes, fear of making, 153
Morale, 61, 138
Mortality and decline on cognitive tests, 16–
    19

N

National Institute of Child Health and
    Human Development, 1, 2
Nervous systems
    central (CNS), 69–72

relation of increased attention to,
    107–123
    heart rate deceleration and, 108–111
    visceral, 72, 77–88
        effect of aging, 77–78
        structure and function, 72, 74–77
Neuro-humoral regulations in aging organ-
    ism, 78–80
New York State Psychiatric Institute, 67
    Life History Interview Schedule, 127–135
    Study of Aging Twins, 13–20
Newman-Keuls multiple-range tests, 34
Norepinephrine, effects of, 72, 73
Nowlin, John B., 70, 107–123, 126
Nutrition, 130

O

Oakland Growth Study, 1, 2
Object Assembly test, 3

P

Perception and intellectual functioning, 152
Performance IQ, 47
Performance skills, 60–61
Personality and intelligence, 45–58, 142
    case history approach, 46
    different patterns of, 53–56
    from infancy to 40 years, 45–58
    Q-sort characteristics, 49–53
        at ages 18, 30, and 40 years, 52
        of persons gaining in IQ, 50
Physical activities, 133
Physiological changes
    behaviorial changes and, 83–105
    effect on attentive states in reaction time,
        107–123
    sex differences, 12
Picture Arrangement tests, 3
Picture Completion tests, 3
Psychological changes in the aging, vi, 132,
    133
    sex differences, 12, 152
    variables influencing, 19

R

Reaction time, 107–116
    adverse effect of age on, 107
    blood pressure changes and, 111–116
    contingent negative variation, 117–122
    effect of physiological changes, vi, 108–
        111

heart rate changes, 108–111
Research, vi
  cross-sectional, 31, 84–85, 146
  data collecting, 154
  longitudinal, vi, 2, 31
  prospects and problems, 149–154
  training investigators, 154
  See also Longitudinal research
Respiration, 111
Rhudick, Paul J., 7–12, 66, 146

S

Schoenfeldt, Lyle F., 31–44, 66
Senescence, 96
  cerebral correlates of intellectual function, 95–105
  chronological age and, 19
Sex differences
  health status, 12
  intellectual ability and, 2–3, 152
  IQ tests, 47, 53
Similarities test, 3
Social isolation factors, 131
Social skills, 47, 56–57
Socioeconomic factors, vi, 19
Somatic variables, vi, 125–126
  cerebral correlates of intellectual function, 95–105
  mechanisms of brain-body interaction, 69–82
  systemic disease and behavioral correlates, 83–93
Speed motor tests, 7, 17, 67, 84
  decline in, 66
Speed of reaction time, 7, 17, 67, 70–71
  Digit Symbol tests, 47, 57
  heart rate and, 108–111, 122–123
  hypertension and, 84
Stanford-Binet tests, 14, 46
Stress, effect of, 132

T

Tapping tests, 14, 17
Terman Group test, 5

Thompson, Larry W., 70, 107–123, 126
Thurnher, Majda, 137–142, 146, 147
Transplant studies, 76–77
Troyer, William G., 69–82, 126
Twins, study of aging, vi, 13–20
  cognitive stability, 67
  differences in degree of aging, 128–129
  interview schedule, 127–135
  present findings, 16–18
  sample, 13–14
  summary of previous findings, 15–16
  testing, 14

V

Verbal abilities, 28
Verbal IQ tests, 47, 65–66
Visceral diseases, 70
Visceral nervous system
  effects of aging on, 77–88
  structure and function, 72, 74–77
Vocabulary tests, 3, 6, 47

W

Wang, H. Shan, 95–105, 126
Wechsler Adult Intelligence Scale (WAIS), 2, 3–4
  blood pressure and intelligence, 83, 86–91
  cerebral blood flow and, 102–104
  comparison of raw scores and age-adjusted, 9
  correlations with Wechsler-Bellevue, 47–49, 57
  Duke ten-year longitudinal study, 22–29
  sex differences, 3–4
  subjects and methods, 8–9
  test and retest scores, 9–10
Wechsler-Bellevue, 3–4, 14, 46
  correlation with WAIS, 47–49, 57
  Form I, 2
  sex differences, 3–4
Weil, Connie, vii
White House Conference on Aging, 64
Wilkie, Frances L., 21–29, 66, 83–93, 126, 146